The Path of the Beatitudes
A New Beginning

The Path of the Beatitudes
A New Beginning

Robert H. Pish

Novem Gradus Press

Novem Gradus Press
San Antonio, Texas

ISBN: 978-0-615-84250-9

© 2002 Robert H. Pish
All Rights Reserved

Library of Congress Control Number: 2013912193

Cover photograph
Franconia Ridge Trail
courtesy of
Bruno Ethier

Printed in the United States of America

The Beatitudes

Blessed are the poor in spirit,
for theirs is the kingdom of heaven

Blessed are they that mourn,
for they shall be comforted

Blessed are the meek,
for they shall inherit the Earth

Blessed are they that hunger and thirst for righteousness,
for they shall be filled

Blessed are the merciful,
for they shall have mercy

Blessed are the pure in heart,
for they shall see God

Blessed are the peacemakers,
for they shall be called children of God

Blessed are they that are persecuted for righteousness sake,
for theirs is the kingdom of heaven

Blessed are you when they insult you and utter every kind of slander against you because of me,
for great is your reward in heaven.[1]

---

[1] Matthew 5:3-12 King James Version - KJV

Table of Contents

Prologue i

Introduction 1

The Beatitudes as a Natural Law 17

The Basic Structure of the Beatitudes 25

    Structure 26

A Brief Overview: A Triad of Triads 33

    The First Triad 33

    The Second Triad 36

    The Third Triad 39

The Structure of Man 45

    The Faculties of Our Human Nature 53

    Personalities 57

Finding a Path 63

On Becoming Vigilant 77

The First Beatitude — Coming Back to the Present 85

The Second Beatitude — Seeing One's Condition 95

A Short Note on Self-Observation 109

The Third Beatitude — A Gift 113

The Fourth Beatitude — Gathering Truth 123

The Fifth Beatitude — Accepting Mercy 135

A Note on Attention 145

The Sixth Beatitude — A Second Greater Gift 151

The Seventh Beatitude — A Call to Peace 161

The Eighth Beatitude — Facing the Sheep and Wolf 177

The Ninth Beatitude — The Search can Begin 183

From the Author 189

    Observations 193

We are like a hand stuck into

a glove at birth.

But we have forgotten that

and believe we are the glove.

… Source unknown

Prologue

A Christian is defined simply as one who follows the teachings of Christ. But the reason for doing so should go far beyond the idea of living a virtuous life so that we might go to heaven when we die. Christ was unambiguous in defining the purpose of his teaching.

> *"It is enough for the disciple that he become like his teacher."*[2]

Christ's call is to become like him in this life: now at this moment in the midst of daily activities and not only in church for one hour a week; not for the few random moments each week when we are reminded to pray or meditate; and not in the future when we imagine that

---

[2] Matthew 10 : 25 NASB, New American Standard Bible

there might be more time to sit quietly and devote more time to our spiritual salvation.

The gospels are full of examples of how Christ lived, his miracles and the works he performed. He provided many parables with pearls of wisdom for those who might come to understand their deeper meaning and many definitions of right and wrong actions. The four gospels indicate that almost all of these were provided to everyone who happened to be around him at the time.

But were there other teachings provided to just his disciples: teachings that were not for the masses: lessons that required a special preparation to understand? Lessons that allowed the apostles to play essential roles in the spreading of Christ's teachings. Lessons for his specially prepared followers who had been given the "ears to hear"

We know that Christ taught and gave his closest disciples the ability to heal the sick and cast out demons but we have little detailed information of what else they were taught in private.[3] In the Gospel of Mark it says…

---

[3] Matthew 10:8; Mark 6:13; Luke 9:1-3; Acts 3:1-9

> ... *they went out and began to go through Galilee, and he did not want anyone to know about it. For he was teaching His disciples ..."* [4]

That section only mentions Christ's prediction of His own impending death and Mark does not offer any other clues to what they might have been taught during this journey through Galilee.

There are two other instances where Christ is specifically teaching only his apostles and perhaps not even all twelve. One was in response to the request to be taught how to pray. Christ gave them what we now call the Lord's Prayer. [5]

Perhaps the most striking example of a special teaching for just his closest disciples occurs with the withdrawal from the crowd to teach his disciples mentioned at the beginning of the Sermon on the Mount. [6]

---

[4] Mark 9:30-31 NASB
[5] Luke 11:1-4 has a short version and Matthew 6:9-13 has the longer more well-known version but without the request by the disciples.
[6] Matthew 5:1-2

The Sermon on the Mount[7] is considered by most scholars to contain the core teachings of Christ, and almost all of the content is what might be called guidelines for right action, activities to avoid and suggestions for activities that an individual wishing to lead a Christian life might undertake at some point in the future. In many respects a list of do's and don't.

The Beatitudes are an exception that does not seem to fit with the rest of this section. They do not appear to fit because rather than suggestions for future "improvements," the Beatitudes speak to conditions that a person is already experiencing — just now. At first glance this seemingly simply set of nine statements most often used to comfort people in times of distress hardly appears to be a closely guarded and privately taught lesson for spiritual development much less a lesson that would be placed first in the Sermon on the Mount. But the parallelism between the nine Beatitudes and the nine statements in the Lord's Prayer seem to be more than an unlikely coincidence and certainly worth more than a passing glance.

---

[7] Matthew Chapters 5-7

With all the available books, lectures, sermons and web sites presenting public and scholarly discussions of the Beatitudes one might suspect that the teachings contained in the Beatitudes have been fairly well exposed over the two millenium since Christ's death, but such is not the case.[8] Certainly, there is value for the many that have benefited from the comforting message of a Beatitude that addressed their current life condition be it persecution, sorrow or other trial with the promise of hope and comfort. And yet there are intriguing clues in the Beatitudes offering great gifts of love such as seeing God, inheriting the earth, and being filled with truth in a world of confusion.

The Beatitudes present a strikingly different role for man than that demanded by the rigid commandments of the Old Testament. Much of the Old Testament defines laws governing things we must not do, and the laws carry a sense of severity. Christ's message, on the contrary, speaks of those things which must be done, and they carry a gift of grace and an overriding sense of love. The Ten Commandments were chiseled into stone and their

---

[8] A cursory survey of the Library of Congress files using the word Beatitudes yielded over 400 titles. A similar search on the Internet listed over 250,000 sites.

mastery came from conforming to external codes and education. Christ's teachings are written on believing hearts by the Holy Spirit and only await our awakening for their manifestation through us.

Some of the earliest writings on the Beatitudes, by Church Fathers[9], mystics, and saints in the first few centuries after Christ, have stated quite directly that the Beatitudes are Christ's statement of the steps necessary for spiritual growth. To them, the Beatitudes were a series of steps which <u>must</u> be followed in sequence for one's spiritual development.

Down through history a few others have written the same message. But while some of these discussions elaborate on the qualities of a person on each step, they generally lack substantive guidance on the preparation and effort necessary to follow what is the essential path of Christianity. And this omission is often an indication that the actual substance of the teachings, the "how" is

---

[9] The Fathers of the Church included theologians, teachers and great bishops though not necessarily "saints", and not necessarily ordained. Their scholarly works set a precedent for understanding Christ's message in the Roman Catholic, Eastern Orthodox, Oriental Orthodox, and Anglican Churches, as well as some other Christian groups.

left for direct person-to-person transmission or some form of Divine enlightenment.

In addition many writers have made the observation that in life a person who chooses to pursue their spiritual development should not expect a continuous and recognizable spiritual growth. The path will be full of twists and turns and more resemble a roller coaster ride or a walk through a labyrinth then a stairway to heaven. Each person will ascend a certain way then fall back to the beginning. Starting over from the beginning many times until the ninth stage is reached which calls to mind a picture of Jacob's Ladder.[10]

But one of the values of the Beatitudes is to remind us that at every moment in our day we have the opportunity to begin again from wherever we are. And we can begin again while doing whatever life demands of us.

It is more than an hypothesis that the teaching of how to strive, the effort required, was reserved for persons specially prepared to receive the deeper meaning of the Beatitudes by their teachers who in their turn had been

---

[10] Genesis 28:12

instructed by their teachers in a long line of oral tradition.

The necessity that this teaching be only available through direct face-to-face transmission[11] would not be unexpected for the preparation and effort required is essentially dependent on the individual. Lacking specific help and preparation based upon the student's specific needs, from one who understands the teaching and also can discern the state of the student in the moment, the task may be almost impossible. And although the question of how may not appear to have a simple answer because there are as many "narrow paths" as there are individuals, Christ's message in the Beatitudes can offer clarity along every path in every religion. For despite the wide variety of religious practices within each religion and between different religions the universality of the law expressed by Christ in the Beatitudes applies to everyone and every path equally. That is exactly what makes the need for a serious study of the Beatitudes so compelling.

~~~

---

[11] Or direct intercession from God

The Bible contains well over three hundred references to man's sleep and the need to awaken. However there is little specific information about what Christ meant by sleep or being awake and no clear information on how we might become awake. But clearly the sleep we are to awaken from is not our normal physical sleep. And being awake implies much more than what is normally considered our waking state in which we spend all of our days. What's more we have been taught — led to believe — that we are already awake and fully conscious. That assumption presents another hurdle that is almost impossible to surmount.

There are also almost four hundred references to man's purpose on earth to seek and to search but little guidance on how to seek.

It is clear that the possibility of awakening and the ability once awake to seek will require some practical guidance for it will involve an exploration of oneself and the world in which we live in an entirely new way. In order to provide a practical way to approach and follow this great teaching of the Beatitudes, it may prove useful to the reader to borrow and test the ideas and methods of other traditions and teachers as they apply directly to this task.

The Biblical references in this book are drawn from various translations because the phrasing of a passage can substantially change or obscure the meaning of a passage. And while most interpretations and discussion of biblical passages are often made in the context of our relation to others and to external events it is also possible to apply many of the same passages to our internal life. As an example, the peacemaker mentioned in the seventh Beatitude can also be seen as one whose spiritual development has led to the possibility of bringing conflicting internal reactions, demands, thoughts and movements into a peaceful state in a moment of presence. When the Beatitudes are applied to one's internal development a new understanding becomes possible.

Additional material from other traditions is included to provide insight into our studies and help us to decipher Christ's message in the Beatitudes by giving a view from a different perspective. Being open to hear the message they contain might prove difficult for some but Christ's message was to become open; like little children; curious and eager to learn ever more using every means possible. But in every case, the aim of all reference material is to assist us to better understand this great teaching of Christ.

The Beatitudes make no attempt to change a person's religion or specific path or practice within a religion or tradition — in fact that is not necessary and in the beginning of our search such changes may even be detrimental because we do not know all of the effects that such changes may have on our further progress.

This book also makes use of a small portion of the work of G. I. Gurdjieff whose very practical approach to human development should prove invaluable to anyone preparing to follow the path of the Beatitudes. His ideas and methods require no beliefs just a simple willingness to verify one's condition for oneself.

Some longtime members of a particular church or religion may question the need for a new beginning feeling that they have been practicing their religion for a very long time and are comfortable in their understanding. But there is often little correlation between external practices performed out of habit and internal or spiritual development. As John C. Wu states:

> *"The reason why so many Christians are frustrated and stunted is that they do not realize the vital importance of continual progress in the spiritual life, and pay but scant attention to the laws of interior growth."* [12]

Of course terms like "continual progress" only leave us with a question of what constitutes progress. Is outside reading, bible study or participation in activities beyond the attendance at weekly services evidence of progress? Perhaps, but perhaps not. These activities may however be evidence of an essential recognition that something is missing and more is desired. Whatever "more" might mean we will see that this God-given desire for "more" is an indiction of a call to awaken.

Unfortunately, many in their search can get lost in trying to explore other religons and philosophies or sample all of the activities available in modern chuches. We must always be on guard against comfortable and enjoyable activities or practices for they can in some cases actually

---

[12] Wu, Obl. O.S.B., J.D., John C. H. "The Interior Carmel: The Threefold Way Of Love" Sheen & Ward, New York, 1953, pg.4.

make our sleep more secure. Such activities can be a very valuable and fulfilling portion of our life but may not necessarily forward our desire to awaken.

~~~

Once seen as a simple and clear statement of the God-given law governing internal growth, the path of the Beatitudes becomes clear. And although allowing ourselves to be led along this path will take considerable time and efforts of a special kind, we can draw comfort from having been shown the way. This journey of inner development is the essential preparation to become able to hear and follow God's plan for each of us. As such following Christ's directions in the Beatitudes should be the central goal of all Christians and members of any religious group.

Perhaps this material, which may only be verified through one's own personal experience, might provide some assistance to all who are searching as we are all after a fashion groping around in the dark and yearning for the light that is only available to those who can awaken.

Introduction

The Sermon on the Mount[13] begins with the statement.

> *When he saw the crowds he went up on the mountainside. After he had sat down his disciples gathered around Him, and he opened His mouth and taught them, saying,*[14]

What follows is the first record of a specific teaching of Christ to his disciples. Some scholars believe that the Sermon on the Mount represents a collection of Christ's teachings that may have been given multiple times to different groups and simply collected into this one area of Matthew's gospel. While this may be true for the bulk

---

[13] The Sermon on the Mount is considered to be Chapters 5, 6 and 7 of the Gospel of Matthew
[14] Matthew 5 : 1-2 KJV, King James Version

Introduction

of the material in the Sermon on the Mount this is not what is indicated in the above statement for the Beatitudes. Jesus went up on the mountain generally indicating a movement away from the crowd and going up a mountain as Moses did often symbolically referred to discussing more important spiritual matters. And his disciples also went "up on the mountain." And following the rabbinic custom of the time Christ sat down and opened his mouth to teach the disciples he had been preparing. There is no indication that it was given to the crowds that had been following Him and listening to His every word despite the sacrifices many in the crowds had made to see him.

St. John Chrysostom writing in the 4th century says...

> But when he had gone up into the mount, and "was set down, His disciples came unto Him." Seest thou their growth in virtue? and how in a moment [or, "all at once"] they became better men? Since the multitude were but gazers on the miracles, but these from that hour desired also to hear some great and high thing. And

Introduction

indeed this it was set Him on His teaching, and made Him begin this discourse.[15]

Christ begins his instruction with the Beatitudes. This placement could be considered to establish the pre-eminence of the Beatitudes in Christ's teaching of spiritual development: for as we shall explore, they define the steps required of all of us.

The Beatitudes

Blessed are the poor in spirit,
　　　　for theirs is the kingdom of heaven
Blessed are they that mourn,
　　　　for they shall be comforted
Blessed are the meek,
　　　　for they shall inherit the Earth
Blessed are they that hunger and thirst for righteousness,
　　　　for they shall be filled
Blessed are the merciful,
　　　　for they shall have mercy
Blessed are the pure in heart,
　　　　for they shall see God

---

[15] St. John Chrysostom (c. 347–407): Homily 15 on St. Matthew: On the Beatitudes, transl. Rev. Sir George Prevost, Bt., 1851, rev. American edition Rev. Matthew B. Riddle, 1888

Introduction

Blessed are the peacemakers,
for they shall be called children of God
Blessed are they that are persecuted for righteousness sake,
for theirs is the kingdom of heaven
Blessed are you when they insult you and utter every kind of slander against you because of me,
for great is your reward in heaven.[16]

St. Augustine [354 to 430], St. John Chrysostom [347 – 407][17], Pope Leo I [c. 391 – 461][18], St. Peter of Damaskos [1027 – abt. 1107][19, 20] and Thomas Aquinas [1225 – 1274][21]

---

[16] Matthew 5 : 3-12 KJV

[17] Archbishop of Constantinople, Doctor of the Church and is generally considered the most prominent doctor of the Greek Church.

[18] Also known as Leo the Great, *Sermon 9: A Homily on the Beatitudes*, From "Nicene and Post-Nicene Fathers, Second Series, Vol. 12," Trans. Charles Lett Feltoe, Christian Literature Publishing Co., Buffalo, NY: 1895.)

[19] *"Philokalia,"* Vol. III, trans. by Philip Sherrard, Faber and Faber, London, p. 93-100.

[20] *The Philokalia* (Gk. "love of the beautiful") is an 18th century compilation by St. Nikodemos of the Holy Mountain and St. Makarios of Corinth of writings for guidance and instruction of monks in "the practise of the contemplative life" of the Eastern Orthodox hesychast tradition between the 4th and 15th centuries. The authors lived before the 11th century schism and their instructions were part of the common heritage of Eastern and Western Christianity,

Introduction

among others affirmed the Beatitudes as the steps a person will make in spiritual development. More than that, they defined these steps as necessary. Each of the nine statements has two parts. The first part describes the characteristics of that stage of spiritual development and the second part, the gift that is given the person who is able to be in that stage even if only for a moment.

St. Theresa of Avila[22] writing around 1577 provides her experiences in each stage of spiritual development without mentioning the Beatitudes. What is striking about her descriptions of the stages is that the sequence in which they are presented accurately matches the sequence of steps contained in the Beatitudes. And while she states that a person might visit the rooms in any order, this may only be because a person in the later stages may pass quickly, almost unnoticeably, through the lower steps. And with each attempt to awaken our progress might stop at any of the steps: sometimes lower sometimes higher. Her personal experiences of the difficulties and rewards of each stage can provide exceptional help for a person on the path of the

---

[21] Aquinas, St. Thomas, "Summa Theologicia" I-II, Q98 Art. 1.
[22] St. Teresa of Avila, "Interior Castle" translated and edited by E. Allison Peers, Image Books, Garden City New York, 1961.

Introduction

Beatitudes. She adds that in her personal experience on the path one will move back and forth thru the stages many times before securing anything permanent.

A few 20th century writers have also discussed the Beatitudes as steps and they have sought to explain each stage.[23,24,25,26,27] This list is not meant to be complete but rather representative.

~~~

Why start from the assumption that such a significant portion of Christ's teaching was given just to the disciples? Even the apostle's questions showed that they did not yet understand the necessity that some of the teachings be reserved for just those who had been prepared to receive them.

---

[23] Wu, Obl. O.S.B., J.D., John C. H. "The Interior Carmel: The Threefold Way Of Love" Sheen & Ward, New York, 1953, pg. 140

[24] Heard, Gerald, "The Code of Christ," Harper and Brothers Publishers, New York, 1941

[25] Heard, Gerald, "The Creed of Christ: An Interpretation of the Lord's Prayer," Wipf and Stock Publishers, Eugene, Oregon

[26] Prabhavananda, Swami, "The Sermon on the Mount According to Vedanta," New American Library, 1972, pg. 17 ff.

[27] Lucado, Max, "The Applause of Heaven," Word Publishing, 1990, Dallas, Tx.

Introduction

> *And the disciples came, and said unto Him, Why speakest thou unto them in parables? He answered and said unto them, "Because it is given unto you to know the mysteries of the kingdom of heaven, but to them it is not given."*[28]

Many people in the crowds that followed Jesus had walked great distances and made other sacrifices to see and hear Him and yet he says.

> *That seeing they may see, and not perceive; and hearing they may hear, and not understand; lest at any time they should be converted, and their sins should be forgiven them.*[29]

These words may seem harsh from Christ who we have been taught came to save all men. But it may only be an indication that some preparation is required before a person will be able to follow this great teaching. Each individual must begin to sense that they are far from what they could be and this is often a very difficult, if not impossible first step for many who already consider

---

[28] Matthew 13 : 10-11 KJV
[29] Mark 4 : 12 KJV

Introduction

themselves good Christians, Jews, Muslims, or members of any other religion or spiritual group. This ability to begin again is made all the more difficult for a person trapped within a rigid set of practices and morals acquired in childhood. But this is the challenge we are given by Christ. And Christ also restated it in the parables of the old and new wineskins,[30] the need for new garments,[31] and the requirements for the rich man.[32]

Religious practices such as mass and sacraments like communion can be extremely valuable in helping us remember our goal, in providing supportive conditions for our search and for the accumulation of grace or [energy] necessary to follow the path of spiritual development when we are in the midst of our daily lives. Other activities such as meditation, fasting and sittings may also support our efforts. But when the purpose of such practices is forgotten, when we attend out of habit and spend most of the time in a distracted state we are seldom open to receive the enormous help that is available. But there is always the hope that continued

---

[30] Matthew 9:17; Mark 2:22; Luke 5:37
[31] Matthew 9:16
[32] Mark 10:17-25

Introduction

participation if only out of habit may in time lead a person to seek to awaken.

Each of us is given many clues and reminders of this need to become more alert or our lack of attentiveness and our almost constant daydreaming. The gift of a faint but certain awareness of an untapped potential, buried by the rush of life, is a call to awaken one's spiritual nature, full consciousness or a connection to one's soul. This call is often sensed as a deep non-verbal awareness that something is missing in one's life — a feeling of separation or aloneness. This call, given to all equally, can remind us of a potential, God-given inheritance that awaits us if we but …

Ah, and there is the catch. What is required of us? Is there a "narrow path" that we must all follow? And if there is only "one true path" why are there so many different religions and different practices within each?

Prayer, fasting, penance, sacred music, physical exercises, pilgrimages, retreats, sacred dances, charitable works, meditation, whirling, study, solitude, intellectual challenges and physical ordeals have been used since ancient times to help develop man's potential higher

Introduction

consciousness or spiritual nature. And many saints and mystics have attained great levels of presence, wisdom, and sanctity by following these diverse methods in different religions and traditions. This implies that one's practices may not be nearly as important as how they are performed or perhaps more accurately how we are when we perform these acts — our state of being or, if you prefer our level of consciousness.

But what is our "level of consciousness?"

We are comprised of two distinct forms of consciousness or at least the possibility of two. These two distinct forms are properties of our two natures: human and spiritual. The first is the one that we consider to be "me." Our human nature is based on our intellectual mind and it gives us our normal perception of ourselves. The spiritual nature can provide a different kind of perception independent of the normal mind that can provide a direct impression of the whole of our self and the universe in which we live. This higher consciousness lies undeveloped in each person awaiting our intentional and active participation in its development. Activation and participation of our spiritual nature in our normal life is the evidence of being awake.

Introduction

Within each consciousness there is a continuum of levels so that the two form a very large range of consciousness possible for man.

Our normal consciousness is comprised of two fundamental attributes; our knowledge [all what we know] and our being [how aware we are in this moment]. In order for anyone to make progress in spiritual development, these two attributes of our normal consciousness need to be balanced before it is possible to awaken the higher form of consciousness. While a person's store of knowledge has been fed since birth, modern culture and education does little to grow our being. As a result of the imbalance of our knowledge and being, the level of this lower consciousness is much less than it could be. And because of this lack of balance we cannot connect to the higher consciousness which is a property of our spiritual nature — our unfulfilled birthright. As a result we function in our lives as partially completed beings.

With but a little reflection on one's own experiences, it is possible to see that for us there is no simple and constant human "being." Our "alertness," our "sensitivity," our "attention," our "level of consciousness" and our "sense

Introduction

of self" varies substantially from day to day, hour to hour and even second to second. And as we are, this "sense of myself" varies without our active participation or awareness. Lacking an active [intentional] awareness of our state, our level of being is primarily controlled by external events or internal automatic processes and most often is at a level far below our rightful state. Recognizing this, one should feel the desire to live in the highest state of being possible in each moment. Religions and religious practices were originally created to help us "improve" our state of being by creating conditions where a person could be more intentional — more conscious. And special rituals and services were designed to offer help to make us more open to the grace — energy — that is awaiting a special kind of willingness necessary to receive. This divine energy or grace in turn has the potential to awaken and allow the exercise of a truly free will where we are not merely slaves to our conditioned, habitual response patterns — even religious ones.

For a person who wishes to awaken, the essential question is how to become more aware in the only moment available to us — just now — and not in some

Introduction

future time when we are not so busy and there are "better" conditions?

This is the message of the Beatitudes which speak to us about this moment.

While we may draw some comfort from the statement that Christ came to save all men, there is that small caveat that many are called but few are chosen.[33] And that statement makes no reference to our role in the process. Christ also states that it is not possible for a person to save himself — it is a gift to those who have been chosen.[34] So that on one hand we are told that Christ has saved us and nothing is required except accepting our salvation.

> *Which of you by worrying can add a single moment to his life-span? If the smallest things are beyond your power, why be anxious about the rest?*[35]

---

[33] Matthew 22 : 14 NAB, New American Bible
[34] Matthew 19: 25-26 NAB
[35] Luke 12:25-26 NAB

Introduction

On the other hand, virtually all of our Western education and practical experience convinces us that everything that we desire in this life requires work, payment — a sacrifice.

> *You know that while all the runners in the stadium take part in the race, the award goes to one man. In that case run so as to win!*[36]

Jeanne de Salzmann defines the paradox that confronts us simply: '*We can do nothing but if we do nothing, nothing can happen.*'[37]

It was in trying to make sense of this paradox that I began. I was not searching so much for a specific path as I was searching for the underlying process that could answer the question of how to get from my normal state to one that was more complete, more balanced, more appropriate for a creature said to have the possibility of residing with God. That has defined my path.

---

[36] 1 Cor. 9:24 NAB
[37] Jeanne de Salzmann, "The Reality of Being" Shambhala Publications, Inc. Boston and London, 2010

Introduction

While I am convinced that man's development does not hinge on knowledge of the Beatitudes or their function in spiritual development, I feel certain that known or not everyone's spiritual progress will follow these steps. The Beatitudes can help us discern what might be required on the path and they show that a considerable effort over perhaps a long time will be required of each of us. And lest we fall prey to the belief that nothing is required of us except a belief in God, Christ's warning is strong.

> *I assure you, unless you change and become like little children, you will not enter the kingdom of God.*[38]

"…unless you change" is a very direct statement that some potentially substantial change is required of us. "…and becoming like little children…" does not appear to be satisfied by a onetime conversion or acceptance of Christ as a savior.

There are many opinions of what it might mean to be like little children but if we cast all the expert opinions aside and simple watch we will see that children [before they become too educated] are curious

---

[38] Matthew 18 : 3 NAB

Introduction

and ready to explore. They lack a fear of the unknown which often accompanies aging and education. They are willing to help others. They are able to accept what they see right now without judgment and also willing to change if later experiences add to or alter their initial perception. And above all they are able to enjoy the moment and express that joy without reservation.

The Beatitudes can guide the changes that will allow us to awaken, become open, to once again become like little children in our appreciation of the great gifts we have received and continue to receive.

Each person who embarks on the path of spiritual development will encounter these steps. Knowing what to expect along the Path of the Beatitudes could prove valuable.

The Beatitudes as a Natural Law

The Beatitudes contain an explanation of a fundamental and universal natural law that not only governs the spiritual development of human beings but also many other physical and psychological processes in the universe. And if we begin to understand this natural law as it manifests in our own personal life we will already understand many of the mysteries of the world around us. The Beatitudes can also provide important clues to the mystery of death and rebirth, the implication of Christ's continual call to awaken and the price of sleep, as well as the idea of what is really required to accept Christ as our personal savior.

The power, elegance and simplicity of the Beatitudes are remarkable among all the writings of all religions. It would not be difficult to argue that the rest of the New

The Beatitudes as a Natural Law

Testament is simply a further explanation and an illustration of a life lived thru the manifestation of one who followed the path of the Beatitudes and the results of not doing so. That this may not be immediately obvious is only an indication that understanding the path of spiritual development contained in the Beatitudes requires a certain preparation. If even a small trip to another city requires preparation and insuring that our vehicle is in good working order, then the journey of a lifetime will take considerable more preparation to insure that our vehicle — our human nature — is in good working order.

But while spiritual development requires the preparation and training of our human nature, this effort is only the groundwork for the awakening and functioning of a completely different nature — our spiritual nature. And though the human nature can easily learn to mimic some actions that may be viewed as spiritual, such actions remain one natured and lack the essence of the divine.

The possibility of existence as a two natured human being may be seen in many Biblical passages.

The Beatitudes as a Natural Law

… glorify God in your body, and in your spirit[39]

"But though our outward man perish, yet the inward man is renewed day by day"[40]

… his flesh upon him shall have pain and his soul within him shall mourn. [41]

Bringing one's spiritual nature or one's soul if you prefer, into active existence and participation in one's *"day by day"* life is the awakening spoken of by Christ. But we cannot assume that our "inward man" is being renewed until such time as our spiritual nature begins to participate in our moment to moment existence: until we are awake.

The steps identified in the Beatitudes are the steps required for both the preparation of the human nature and the awakening and development of our spiritual nature. However, the preparation and the continuing effort required to move up these steps — the answer to

---

[39] 1 Cor. 6:20 KJV, King James Version
[40] 2 Cor. 4:16 KJV
[41] Job 14:22 KJV

The Beatitudes as a Natural Law

the question of how — does not have a universal, "one-size-fits-all" answer.

There can be no universal method of preparation, for each of us represents a unique set of preexisting experiences, beliefs, education, habits and personalities. In addition, each of us tends to rely more heavily on one of the three primary faculties of the human nature: intellect, emotions, body. And research has shown that we start on this path with many deeply engrained beliefs about what will work and what will not. Were teachers who had completed the path available in sufficient numbers, their experience, perceptions and wisdom could prove invaluable in guiding us along these diverse paths. But this is the "few" spoken of earlier. Lacking such real teachers, it might be possible for a small group of serious people with the assistance of a person who is already on the path to work together.

Married or single, monk or minister, cleric or lay person there is the possibility of acquiring a connection to one's spiritual nature as real as the singular human nature where we spend all of our days. We feel the earth under our feet support our weight as we walk and are confident in our human nature but we seldom feel the

The Beatitudes as a Natural Law

support which is just as present, just a real for our as yet unawakened spiritual nature. In this possibility of awakening our spiritual nature, all of us are created equally. All are given experiences of a few moments in life that are much more vivid leaving bright intense memories that stand out from dim recollections of yesterdays. These bright moments are the taste of a higher state of existence possible for each of us. They are not only verification that we could exist in a much more conscious way but are also a part of Christ's call to awaken. And despite the mind's normal acceptance and explanation of these moments as merely being slightly more alert than normal they are if fact experiences of an entirely different order.

There is a story which exists in several traditions and many forms and dates back into the distant past.

> *There once was a person who went to his church each day around noon and knelt in prayer for two hours or more. He had done this for years never missing a day even when he was ill. One day in frustration he cries out in the empty church "My God, I have come here to pray every day for more than 30 years and*

The Beatitudes as a Natural Law

you have never once spoken to me. Why do you not speak to me?"

In the stillness of the empty church, a voice softly replies "I came to you 6,000 times yesterday but you were busy and did not hear me."

In our one-natured existence the call is seldom heard: but in quieter moments, we may have heard the call and failed to recognize it in the din of our normal, one-natured existence: we were and are asleep.

All great religions were created to support man's effort to answer the call and help men gain access — become open to receive — a permanent connection to their free will, soul, conscience and consciousness — a connection to a spiritual or higher nature — and hopefully beyond. And although the language and methods differ greatly around the world and down through time, the underlying processes involved follow natural laws: the law outlined in the Beatitudes.

The first step will remain the same for all: recognition that we were created as incomplete or partial beings with only one active nature. Or more simply viewed and

The Beatitudes as a Natural Law

experienced, we are not all that we could be. It has been said that the range of consciousness and being possible for a person varies from that of the simplest animal to that of the angels. Existing with only one functioning nature limits us to just the lowest part of the range available. Even in that limited area, awareness and sensitivity [the level of consciousness or being] is continually rising and falling as a result of outer and inner activities and surroundings. To live such a one-natured existence, acquiescing to our conditioned responses is to accept a life unbecoming to a creature created by God to inherit immortality.

The Beatitudes represent the nine steps for preparing our human nature and developing one's spiritual nature regardless of the path, practice or religion chosen. That possibility alone should warrant a serious study of the Beatitudes.

The Beatitudes as a Natural Law

The Basic Structure of the Beatitudes

Before exploring the nine Beatitudes in detail, it can be valuable to look at the beauty, eloquence and simplicity of the structure of the Beatitudes and to take a moment for a quick overview of the nine statements. Once seen, the efforts called for in these steps should be familiar to all church going Christians. And the Beatitudes may even resonate more deeply because they reflect a universal law that governs not only our spiritual development but how all of our activities and projects develop in time. Once studied and experienced, the steps and processes identified in the Beatitudes begin to move a person from a life based on what we have been told — our beliefs — to one based on the evidence from our own personal experiences — our faith. And this can continue to grow into a life of faith that can move mountains.

The Basic Structure of the Beatitudes

In the words of St. John Chrysostom in the 4th Century,

> *It is not without reason that the beatitudes are disposed of in this order. Each preceding one prepares the way for what immediately follows, furnishing us in particular with spiritual arms of such graces as are necessary for obtaining the virtue of the subsequent beatitude. Thus the poor in spirit, i.e. the truly humble, will mourn for their transgressions, and whoever is filled with sorrow and confusion for his own sins, cannot but be just, and behave to others with meekness and clemency; when possessed of these virtues, he then becomes pure and clean of heart. Peace of conscience reigns in this assemblage of virtues, and cannot be expelled from the soul by any tribulations, persecutions, or injustices of men.*[42]

Structure

A few writers have noted that the Beatitudes fall conveniently into three groups of three statements as do the nine statements in the Lord's Prayer and both for the same purpose: to show and lead in the work of gathering

---

[42] St. John Chrysostom, Homily xv. Doctor of the Church, born at Antioch, c. 347; died 14 September, 407

The Basic Structure of the Beatitudes

for oneself more direct experiences in this moment. This grouping in three parts is a reflection in our lives of another universal law that is evidenced in what is called the Mystery of the Holy Trinity.[43]

Each triad of the Beatitudes begins with the recognition of a need or lack: Beatitudes 1, 4, and 7. Each continues the effort of gathering experiences: Beatitudes 2, 5, and 8. And the third Beatitude in each triad, not only marks the completion of that triad but does so with an exceptional gift: Beatitudes 3, 6 and 9.

One may also notice that the nine Beatitudes are comprised of seven Beatitudes where it seems that some effort [perhaps realization is a better word] is required and two intermediate Beatitudes where a significant change of state is given as a gift [3 and 6]. The seven, we might call working Beatitudes, are a chance to understand why the number seven figures so prominently in mystical and spiritual writings.

> *An appreciation of the significance of the number seven pervades Augustine's*

---

[43] It is appropriate to consider all natural laws as evidence of the divine creative process that manifests in all aspects of our lives.

The Basic Structure of the Beatitudes

presentation. In his mind the number seven signified plenitude, perfection and completeness. It was a holy and sacred number. Speaking in various places about the special import of seven, He explicitly links the number with the Holy Spirit [44]

The biblical references to the number seven also indicate the nature of the process of spiritual development. These steps as stated in the Beatitudes are a clear presentation of the universal law that governs all natural processes and the steps that will be encountered if we begin to follow Christ's direction in the Beatitudes.

The promises of the Lord are sure, like tried silver, freed from dross, sevenfold refined.[45]

For the just man falls seven times and rises again[46]

---

[44] cf. Tractate CXXII, n. 8, *On the Gospel of John*. Van Lier, Doctor of the Church, born at Antioch, c. 347; died at Commana in Pontus, 14 September, 407de, C., *Doctrina Sancti Augustini circa Dona Spiritus Spiritus Sancti ex Textu Is XI: 2-3* (Angelicum, Rome, 1935), pp. 49-50.

[45] Psalm 12 : 7 NAB

[46] Proverbs 24 : 16 NAB

The Basic Structure of the Beatitudes

Out of six troubles he will deliver you and at the seventh no evil shall touch you.[47]

These Old Testament quotes indicate the nature and significance of a lawful but unexplained process made explicit by Christ in the Beatitudes. Six times we have to overcome some obstacle. Six times we are subject to the <u>necessity</u> of the loss of everything for only "at the seventh no evil shall touch you." And what seems the most significant indication is that only after seven trials, are we given permanency. At each step or stage of development, we will be melted down and reformed — "refined." Until the entire process is completed we may lose everything and this indicates that the steps of spiritual development will be started over from the beginning time and again until we are able to reach the ninth step. And while the idea of slowly becoming a better person is correct, it may be far different process and more difficult than most believe.

But as an example of the universality [lawfulness] of the seven steps required completing any project, we are given the creation story in Genesis as the very first

---

[47] Job 5 : 19 NAB

The Basic Structure of the Beatitudes

story.[48] Why would we be told that it God took seven 'days' to create the world and did not rest until the seventh day when the creation was completed? Surely God did not need seven days or even seven steps of any length and since God should not need to rest, 'rest' implies completion. And while the origins of the seven day week remain uncertain in the literature, it may well be a reflection of the natural law contained in the Beatitudes in much the same way scientific data was encoded in paintings, music and the architecture of great monuments.

This structure is also represented symbolically in sacred art of many traditions by a triangle inscribed in a circle.

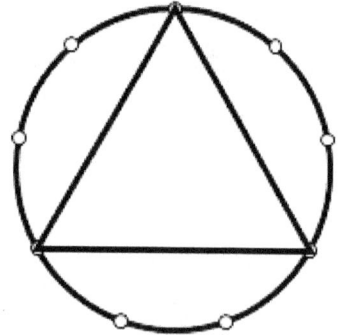

---

[48] Genesis 1 – 2 : 2-4

The Basic Structure of the Beatitudes

Symbols are a means of transmitting information that can bypass the normal intellect and penetrate more directly and deeply into other faculties. They have the ability to carrying meaning without words and truth that bypasses the normal intellect.

One interpretation of the symbol [and there are many other equally valid ways to use/see this symbol] is that the triangle represents the Trinity within the Singular Divine Being represented by the circle. But for our purposes it can also be seen to represent the three elements or forces that may come together in a fully-realized, two-natured human being.

The Basic Structure of the Beatitudes

If we place the Beatitudes around this circle, we see that the vertices of the triangle coincide with the 3rd, 6th, and 9th Beatitudes. This triad represents the essential forces that are a part of a fully developed person [9th Beatitude] accepting life on earth [3rd Beatitude] under the direct influence of God in this moment [6th Beatitude]. The perimeter of the circle represents the process in time to reach this state. The location of the remaining six Beatitudes around the perimeter of the circle, define the stages in a person's growth.

A Brief Overview: A Triad of Triads

The First Triad

Thomas Aquinas[49] and St. John of the Cross[50] call this the triad of purgation. The first two Beatitudes indicate a certain effort to know oneself and an increasing level of recognition of one's condition. Seeing that we spend the vast majority of our day caught in habits reacting to external events we begin to be purged — cleansed — of the belief that we are awake and have a functioning free will. This is the beginning of our death in the sense of the Biblical death and rebirth.[51] Given the grace to persist, the third Beatitude can open us to the entire Earth.

---

[49] Aquinas, St. Thomas, "Summa Theologicia" I-II, Q98 Art. 1.
[50] St. John of the Cross, "Dark Night of the Soul"
[51] John 3: 3-7; Matthew 16:24-25; Mark 8:34-35; Romans 6:4-8;

A Brief Overview: A Triad of Triads

> *1] Blessed are the poor in spirit, for theirs is the kingdom of heaven*

We will not make efforts to obtain anything in life or beyond until we begin to sense that we have an unfulfilled desire, an unanswered question or simply a feeling that something is lacking. This Beatitude is about beginning to recognize our condition just in this moment and has nothing to do with making oneself poor. As St. John Chrysostom says ...

> *"Thus he said not, Blessed are you, if you become poor, but Blessed are the poor."*[52]

This Beatitude implies that seeing that we are not as we could be in this moment merits a rather amazing gift but raises the question of how to see for it does not imply a simple or one-time intellectual or emotional acceptance.

> *2] Blessed are they that mourn, for they shall be comforted*

---

[52] St. John Chrysostom: Homily 15 on St. Matthew: On the Beatitudes, transl. Rev. Sir George Prevost, Bt., 1851, rev. American edition Rev. Matthew B. Riddle, 1888

A Brief Overview: A Triad of Triads

If the repeated experience that something is missing begins to spread within us and we notice it more frequently, we will begin to actually feel an increasing sense of lack — we mourn for what we do not have. We have all experienced this form of discomfort or sadness in life due to an unfulfilled wish whether it was for a car, new shoes or health. How much more should we mourn for a lack of connection to our higher nature? But this mourning is not negative. It is the beginning of a deep longing for that which we are missing. As the discomfort deepens, we are told that it will not be unbearable for we will be comforted. The mourning will continue as we attempt to satisfy the discomfort perhaps trying many different methods and even searching thru different religions and traditions. Accepting to be vigilant long enough for that process to be completed in oneself is part of the process by which we may be made meek.

3] Blessed are the meek, for they shall inherit the Earth

The discomfort experienced in the second Beatitude will grow until we recognize with all of our being — organically — that we cannot advance our state through our own efforts. This process will take different lengths

A Brief Overview: A Triad of Triads

of time depending on the strength of our ego, vanity and pride as manifest in habits and defended knowledge and beliefs. If we can acquire sufficient personal experience that proves we do not have the knowledge or skill to advance our state and we cannot acquire a connection to God thru our own efforts, the world opens. We will have moved from the rigid beliefs that block our opening to a more porous existence with the capability of accepting guidance.

The Second Triad

Thomas Aquinas defined the second three Beatitudes to be those of active happiness. St. John of the Cross defines this stage as the stage of Illumination.[53] In his book on the Beatitudes, John Wu refers to this triad as the Stage of Illumination and the Age of Proficients wherein love blossoms.[54] Gerald Heard calls the fourth and fifth

---

[53] St. John of the Cross, "Dark Night of the Soul"
[54] Wu, John C. H., Obl. O.S.B., J.D., "The Interior Carmel: The Threefold Way of Love" Sheed & Ward, New York, 1953, pg. 105

A Brief Overview: A Triad of Triads

Beatitudes the steps of Proficiency and the sixth Beatitude the one of Perfection.[55]

> *4] Blessed are they that hunger and thirst for righteousness, for they shall be filled*

Having been made open, we will be willing to listen and accept the truth in which we are immersed. Fixed ideas, beliefs and rigid notions begin to fall away in moments of being awake, as we eagerly feed on new impressions that are no longer filtered and stripped of their real value by the automatic interpretations and response of our ego, beliefs, memories and habits. Having been temporarily opened in the third Beatitude we will hunger and thirst for more of this "fresh" truth that can free us from our partiality and give us a sense of what Gerald Heard calls *right-wise-ness* or a feel for what is needed and appropriate in this moment. This Beatitude promises that we will be filled.

> *5] Blessed are the merciful, for they shall have mercy*

---

[55] Heard, Gerald "The Code of Christ" Harper and Brothers Publishers, New York, 1941

A Brief Overview: A Triad of Triads

Having paid the price thru our own effort to be made open and filled with the truth of what we see, we become aware that not everyone has been given such a great opportunity and so many unmerited gifts. We will become more tolerant of those around us that at some point might have received our anger or negative judgments. And exactly like the 2nd Beatitude this step will vary greatly in duration as some will take much longer to become merciful to others and perhaps much longer to be able to accept mercy.

> *6] Blessed are the pure in heart, for they shall see God*

Even a modest amount of introspection will prove that we are very far from being "pure in heart." If we have reached this stage, we also understand it to be unattainable through our own effort. So this step is most certainly a gift like the process in the 3rd Beatitude of being made meek. When we have spent sufficient time in earlier stages we may begin to experience the first glimpses of an opening into …

Here it is better to leave the 'open into what' as an unknown, for to define its form or to say how God might

A Brief Overview: A Triad of Triads

manifest would be to limit and even block our availability.

The Third Triad

The final triad is the most obscure and little is written about it perhaps because so few reach this stage of development or are able to write about it in a form that those of us not yet on the path may recognize. Most often sermons focus on the meaning of these Beatitudes in relation to our interaction with others. But these three stages will be seen to continue to refer to our inner development.

> *7] Blessed are the peacemakers, for they shall be called children of God*

Only those who have been made pure in heart — in this moment — have the capacity to be peacemakers — in this moment; Able to stand between opposing views and accept and reconcile where possible. This is first and foremost an internal peacemaking. Very young children before they are given a rigid moral code for everything have this ability to allow what is happening in the moment to be observed and react in a natural way. Later

A Brief Overview: A Triad of Triads

their education will provide the distraction of differing views, memories and actions arising from inside. In this Beatitude we are told we shall again be freed from our fixed ideas that have for so long biased and constrained our lives.

> *8] Blessed are they that are persecuted for righteousness sake, for theirs is the kingdom of heaven*

The problem with being a true peacemaker is that both sides assume that you are favoring the opponent. The Beatitudes point to this as an internal confrontation. One part wants us to act the way we have been taught is "more correct" — more right. This is most often an automatic manifestation of our lower nature. Other automatic habits and desires also arising from our lower nature pull us in opposite directions. In a certain way, it does not matter which wins since they are both mechanical habitual responses. But with a more developed sense of presence we may be able to also have an opening to other more appropriate actions provided from our higher nature. This capability was manifest in Christ responses when questioned by the Pharisees who

A Brief Overview: A Triad of Triads

in their one-natured existence assumed there were only two possible answers.

> *"Teacher, ... Tell us then, what do You think? Is it lawful to give a poll-tax to Caesar, or not?" But Jesus perceived their malice, and said, "Why are you testing Me, you hypocrites? Show Me the coin used for the poll-tax." And they brought Him a denarius. And He *said to them, "Whose likeness and inscription is this?" They *said to Him, "Caesar's." Then He said to them, "Then render to Caesar the things that are Caesar's; and to God the things that are God's." And hearing this, they were amazed, and leaving Him, they went away.*[56]

This stage requires a constant balancing act between the conflict arising from internal and external forces sustained by the separately functioning parts of our human nature and the pull of our spiritual nature. While in this life our charge is to sheppard both — enduring the negative manifestations and conflicts. And it will often be a real internal battle with biased logic, habitual

---

[56] Matthew 22:15-22 NASB

A Brief Overview: A Triad of Triads

judgments, fear, wishful thinking and all trying to overcome the other views. And like the 2nd and 5th stage, we will remain in this stage until we have been sufficiently prepared.

> *9] Blessed are you when they insult you and utter every kind of slander against you because of me, for great is your reward in heaven*

The ninth and final Beatitude shows that the acceptance of this inner "persecution" and perhaps external persecution to be the price of our freedom and the permanency of our two natured existence. It is the stage in our development where we will be given the guidance and energy, the grace and capability to learn God's plan for us. And we will have been given the capacity to follow it.

Without making this journey through the steps of the Beatitudes we will still fulfill a part of our purpose as members of another species of one-natured animals that support the eco-system by eating and breathing to exchange one chemical compound for another and by reproducing our species. But we have been given a

A Brief Overview: A Triad of Triads

possible inheritance of much more ... if we can but awaken and accept it.

What is clear is that until we reach the last step, nothing is permanent. Like the illustration of Jacob's ladder, a person on Christ's path will continually be moving up or back down — having to start over from the bottom.[57] This is the challenge. Each of us has been put into this life on earth and given the opportunity to accept growth with the entire earth and life situations as what might be called our unique conditions for the development of our soul.

---

[57] Genesis 28:12

A Brief Overview: A Triad of Triads

The Structure of Man

The Beatitudes contain a surprisingly clear map showing the stages of development of what may be called a fully realized human being comprised of two natures: One human and one spiritual or divine nature.

> *Just as we have borne the image of the earthy, we will also bear the image of the heavenly. Now I say this, brethren, that flesh and blood cannot inherit the kingdom of God; nor does the perishable inherit the imperishable.*[58]

This quote states that as we are, we do not yet have the 'image of the heavenly' and then adds urgency to the need to awaken as it indicates that existence after death will depend on the awakening of an imperishable

---

[58] 1 Corinthians 15:49-50 NASB

The Structure of Man

spiritual nature and not just the improvement of the human nature.

There is an ancient parable that also carries the same message: We need to awaken to our role as a being responsible for the care not only of all that we currently call ourselves but also to the spiritual nature which is our unawakened heritage.

> *Only he will deserve the name of man and can count upon anything prepared for him from Above, who has already acquired corresponding data for being able to preserve intact both the wolf and the sheep confided to his care.*[59]

One interpretation of this story is that the sheep and the wolf are a man's two natures. Many struggle under the assumptions that the goal is to become the sheep and live with the spiritual nature in control. For this, one would have to train the sheep to overpower and control the wolf and clearly that is not possible although many try. In life sheep are the most easily frightened and docile

---

[59] Gurdjieff, G.I., Meetings with Remarkable Men, E. P. Dutton & Company 1963, pg. 4

The Structure of Man

creatures. In short, experience proves that left to themselves, the wolf will always wind up with a full stomach. This saying implies that what is required is to protect and support the growth of the sheep [our spiritual nature] and be ever vigilant of the wolf [our human nature].

Our responsibility for two natures also appears quite plainly in St. Paul's letter to the Galatians.

> *The flesh lusts against the spirit and the spirit lusts against the flesh; the two are directly opposed.*[60]

We are called to awaken to our essential role as the being entrusted with the care of these two natures. For this, we must have an attention capable of keeping vigilance over both natures at the same time and this requires a connection to our higher nature with its faculties not just in certain moments set aside for prayer or meditation. Without constant vigilance the wolf comprised of ego driven personalities and habitual actions will have free reign over our lives the majority of each day. This vigilance maintained with a clear attention must become

---

[60] Galatians 5:17 NAB

The Structure of Man

strong enough to be a constant factor in our life and this matches the call in various traditions to pray continually and Christ's call to the apostles to stay awake.

Again the question is how.

Preparation for the journey of a lifetime — to claim a spiritual connection — cannot be accomplished with only the normal intellect or emotions no matter how advanced a person considers themselves. Each of us was created with the potential to connect to our higher nature which has other as yet undeveloped faculties. But without direct personal experience of this we continue to submit to thoughts and emotions as though they were somehow essential to our well-being. They are not. They are only a small part of what we call ourselves under the label of "I" and until we can begin to sense the whole of ourselves in the moment — our presence — we will have no way to comprehend the role of each part.

This desire to be able to sense the whole of ourselves will have little value if it is only accepted intellectually or emotionally. And any view of ourselves through these small parts of our lower nature will only add to our ego-centric, self-deception: A deception that leads each of us

The Structure of Man

to expect some great result from even the smallest action or prayer. It is that expectation generated in our mind that blocks our perception and participation in the truth, the reality here and now. For the normal mind is the home of ego — the chief obstacle to awakening. We need to see [personally verify by our own experience] that our search for truth is defeated from the beginning because we define its objective and by so doing limit our vision to just that expected result. To rely only on the words and partially digested experience of others is a path which can lead to nowhere.

> *When one tastes a fruit one can describe the experience of what one ate, and how one ate in great detail but the essence of eating, the taste itself, cannot be described or defined – that is something one has to find out for oneself. So it is written: "taste and see that God is good."* [61,62]

But how could we allow all that we think and feel to be ignored or abandoned? Would there be anything left to

---

61 Psalm 34:8
62 Rabbi Adin Steinsaltz, "The New Year." Parabola Magazine, Fall 2008. Rabbi Steinsaltz is one of the world's leading Talmudic scholars

The Structure of Man

fill the void? Just the thought of this can bring fear: the fear of being alone and in the dark — vulnerable — without our habits and factoids[63] to protect us. And we do not suspect that all of our stored and recalled knowledge is not truth. For truth is alive and exists in this moment. Stored impressions represent only partial filtered and altered glimpses from the past that lack essence and energy.

But is it even possible to remove our automatically arising thoughts and emotions?

The answer could not be simpler or more difficult to achieve. We cannot discard our thoughts and emotions. We must accept to see them as a part of ourselves but only a small part. Today we see ourselves with one of these small parts watching and judging another small part. And all of this taking place after the event. We have no sense of the whole of ourselves in the moment and so each partial impression is distorted, filtered and justified by the existing preconceptions of the personality that is in charge in the moment. The essence of the observation,

---

[63] Factoid, something taken to be a truth without personal verification

The Structure of Man

the real energy of the impression that could feed our growth is almost completely lost.

But there are hints passed down from antiquity in all religions and cultures. Seng Ts'an in the tradition of Zen Buddhism[64] about the year 540 provides a caution.

> *Do not abide in dualistic views; Take care not*
> *to seek after them.*
> *As soon as there is right and wrong the mind*
> *is scattered and lost.* [65]

And this is simply another way of repeating Christ's direction not to judge. Perhaps this is why a sunrise or sunset can be so breathtaking — we have no right or wrong image and the pure wonder and beauty of the impression can occasionally sink very deep within us — not caught and dissected by our superficial functions. Of course that beauty perceived in the moment starts to diminish as soon as we compare it to other sunrises or

---

[64] The Japanese word Zen is derived from the Chinese word Chán, which in turn is derived from the Sanskrit word dhyāna, which can be approximately translated as "meditation" or "meditative state". Wikipedia

[65] Seng Ts'an, the Third Patriarch of Chan[65] in his poem *Faith Mind*.

The Structure of Man

start trying to explain it to others. Often when we have tried to explain some wonderful event or impression we actually can sense the hollowness of the words we are trying to use and feel our inability to share the experience.

In the beginning, it is difficult to observe oneself without at least some idea of one's inner structure. For this, the system presented by G. I. Gurdjieff can offer some clarity. He states that each person has three primary faculties each with their own function, habits and set of memories not often accessible to the other functions: The intellect located in the head brain; the emotions distributed throughout the nervous system and the body functions centered in the spinal column. Each faculty or center operates at a different speed and each requires a different quality of food which the chemical factory of the body can produce from physical food, air and impressions. But in addition to providing the right food for these three functions, the body also has the capacity to generate much finer chemicals that are the foods that can feed the higher faculties of the spiritual nature. But these higher and what we might call spiritualized foods can only be produced in a person who is awake.

The Structure of Man

The Faculties of Our Human Nature

The intellect operates with words and its automatic part is the source of the internal dialog that plays streams of thought continuously. While the primary function of the intellect is to weigh options, its automatic function is purely a stimulus response mechanism where any word, external event or internal movement can divert the current string of thoughts to a new subject and a different string of automatic thoughts. In addition, the new impressions cause an automatic recall of associated memories, opinions, and names that once recalled often replace the new impression with an old established internal word. We see a beautiful tree and our automatic system says "oak" and the fresh impressions coming from the outside become a muddle of past recollections and fragmented new impressions. In the end the wonder seen in the moment is replaced by what might be called a hodgepodge of mixed memories. And in a very short time we cease to even notice the actual tree as we pass.

This automatic recalling of stored and often distorted impressions to compare, modify and replace new impressions can become that blinding that we do not even notice the space around us; it having been

The Structure of Man

automatically ignored or labeled and dismissed. The result is that we most often live in a state of identification existing within our stored memories rather than in reality. With but a little self-observation we will see that our normal thoughts are a separate, automatic and habitual activity in many ways like our blood flow. We will come to see that the part that is doing the continuous thinking, our mind, is not "I" and in fact, our obsession with and belief in "my thoughts" stands as an obstacle to the awakening of our real "I" for the unknown cannot be approached with the knowledge we have accumulated in life.

To perform the function for which it was designed, the weighing of options, the intellect requires both a positive and a negative part and a certain quality and quantity of attention. Fortunately, we have a small amount of attention that we can learn to control and it is sufficient for our daily lives and can be used to begin our observations until the higher part of us that contains the real observer can be awakened.

The emotional center does not work with words but tends to work with pictures, sounds or images. In its highest function it has the ability to appreciate beauty

The Structure of Man

and truth. However it operates almost totally from its automatic part and is constantly beset by preprogrammed likes and dislikes learned from childhood. The emotions function at a much higher speed than the intellect and experience will show that the "feelings" are formed almost instantly as a result of some outer or inner event. The physical body also working very fast begins to react almost immediately by adjusting the chemistry and muscle system to meet the emotional perception. Much later, on this time scale, the intellect catches up, often being the part relegated to explaining the emotional play or justifying its actions. The automatic arising of likes and dislikes indicates that the emotional center also has a negative and positive part.

The physical or body center contains the functions necessary for movement and for the formation of complex motor skills. In addition the body also contains two more functions: instinctive and sex-creative. The body functions at a much higher speed than the intellect allowing the body to react to danger or changing conditions long before the intellect can recognize the danger or respond. The physical body can learn complex physical tasks and quickly establishes habits of posture

The Structure of Man

and movement which in later times may be very hard to change.

These centers have had virtually no training in cooperation and communication between themselves. The small attention of each center is often attracted by or towards different sensations at the same time. This divided activity called identification defines our state of waking sleep and maintains our being at a very low level. The small attentions of these three faculties, automatically drawn outward, allow our energy to flow outward, away from us, in different directions as well. This not only brings the tension that consumes our available energy, but also captivates and distracts us from the wish to look inward — to be more present. Bringing such disparate faculties into a proper balance so that they might support our wish is a non-trivial task that is "almost" impossible. However, with real self-observation — the vigilance called for in the Bible — we may in time be made opened and brought into a balanced state of being where sensations are perceived by all three centers at the same time and each center can function as required in the moment. This is a dynamic balance changing as conditions change in the moment. At times one center may be required to lead and another

The Structure of Man

to remain still with the roles reversing in the next moment. But for now we will simply see that each center operates independently and as a result of outside stimuli or inner automatically arising impulses. But we do not notice or control these processes.

Personalities

Overlaying this fundamental triune structure is a system of learned stimulus-response patterns — personalities. A typical well educated human might have as many as one or two dozen personalities. These personalities help us exist in different social, business, religious and family activities. These personalities are very useful for life on earth to provide quick and automatic answers and defenses in different conditions. For that purpose most personalities can be beneficial for one-natured beings. But because these personalities react in our name without any intentional participation they also maintain our sleep. Over time our stimulus-response patterns can completely envelop every situation and block spiritual development. In that sense many personalities can also be called *evil*. Left unchecked, each of us will

The Structure of Man

unconsciously continue to solidify this rigid set of personalities making a hard shell of habits, beliefs and illusions. This shell isolates and protects us from reality. And if we have been educated responsibly, the habits will anchor us in what we have been taught are good habits, allowing us to retreat into a life of safe practices with minimal challenges.

Each personality is a certain learned automatic arrangement of one or more of the three centers. One might be predominantly intellectual, rational with little emotion. Another might be skilled in some very complex physical tasks but without any requirement for thought or understanding about the inner operation or its reasons. And still others are primarily emotional with little rational capability but some physical support. Under certain conditions a person might be quite intellectual and only seconds later be consumed by emotional reactions. Self-observation would not be so complicated or take so long if the personality in charge was not constantly changing. Changes occur frequently sometimes shifting every couple of minutes or even quicker in response to changing conditions. Each associative thought, emotion, external event or internal sensation can shift us to a new personality most often

The Structure of Man

without our being aware of the shift. Something as slight as a noise or a breeze across the skin or the sight of another person can cause an instant shift to a new personality. But we have been taught the pronoun "I" and through its repeated use when in different personalities the illusion that we are always one and the same person with a certain set of beliefs has been habituated in us. But this "I" is not a singularity. Each personality has its own individual habits, postures, memories, vocabulary and modified version of a moral code. In many cases these attributes and especially its memories often remain locked within only one personality, not accessible while we are in another personality. It is in this sense that we could quite accurately answer that our name is "legion."[66]

The problem is that we fail to see our existence as partial creatures and we are unaware of our real possibilities. Science has only recently become convinced that the universe that we can see and measure with our best telescopes and instruments is less than 5 percent of the matter and energy that exists. Science calls the 95% of the universe that we cannot see dark energy and dark

---

[66] Mark 5:9

The Structure of Man

matter. And using the old wisdom *'as above so below'* attributed to the Emerald Tablet of Hermes Trismegistus we might apply that to our limited knowledge of ourselves.[67] Perhaps if we travel the path of the Beatitudes we will come to see that in our sleep we were blocked from seeing more than 95 percent of our potential God-given inheritance.

In this state of identification any energy that could have been used to awaken is spent on automatically arising associations, programmed emotional reactions, and unnecessary tensions and movements in the body.

But how can we come to know our willing submission to the control of our lower nature when our experience shows that we prefer to obey the automatic impulses that arise from old stored associations, ideas and habits and for the most part, we are afraid to do otherwise?

We will remain a willing slave to our lower nature as long as we continue to listen to and believe our ego-

---

[67] Nicholas Goodrick-Clarke. The Western Esoteric Traditions: A Historical Introduction. Oxford University Press, 2008. p. 34.

The Structure of Man

centric "I am right" or "That is just the way I am." We must try to resist the dictates of the automatically arising reactions to external and internal stimuli. For only in the struggle to see our slavery to our fears and habits, our thoughts and beliefs, is there a chance for awakening. This struggle begins with the initial step on the path of the Beatitudes.

The Structure of Man

Finding a Path

In order to follow the steps of the Beatitudes, it is almost a rule that we must find a path or religious practice to support, encourage and assist our efforts, for without support, help and guidance it will be nearly impossible. Many of us will have been "born into" a path, a religion to which we have remained faithful. Some will have explored several paths. All major religions and schools of spiritual development offer multiple paths that allow an individual to find a practice that appears appropriate to them. Christianity and in particular the Catholic Church is a good example of a religion with very many possible paths from religious orders that are cloistered to those involved in ministries ranging from health care to education to groups for single, married, senior and youth members. And although the practices along the available

Finding a Path

paths differ widely they can be related to four basic approaches.

As mentioned previously, a person with only one nature is composed of three fundamental parts: intellect, emotion and body. And in their origins, the three most common paths tend to emphasize development of one of these parts although there are many combinations that now exist.

The original schools of Yoga were often methods by which a person sought to develop will and attention thru intense intellectual activity and study. The path of Yoga took many years and intense effort but with persistence the student might acquire an exceptionally developed intellect, strong will and force of attention. Many saints and mystics have started in the scholarly schools of Christianity, Judaism and Yoga.

The monastic schools were fundamentally an approach based upon the belief that ordinary life situations presented too many challenges to staying God-centric and most of the distractions were to a person's emotions. The theory being that within a monastery or hermitage, emotional challenges could be reduced and the monk

Finding a Path

apprentice could lead a simple life devoted to prayer and physical work. Saints Benedict, Bernard and Theresa of Avila among many others were products of this path whose lives although cloistered have influenced mankind's perception of mysticism[68] and spirituality for countless generations.

The path of development thru the body is best typified by the schools of the fakirs in India and the some Moslem dervishes. Students of the Sufi Order of Mevlevi dervishes known as the whirling dervishes were able to turn in place for long periods of time and reach elevated states of awareness typical of the states of ecstasy experienced in other religions and schools. Some fakirs attained great will power and control by as an example holding one arm outstretched for months and perhaps even years. Often these fakirs maintained their posture for so long that their joints stiffened and they could not move without assistance from others. But the power of their will allowed them to develop and demonstrate miraculous feats.

---

[68] Mysticism (Greek *mystikos*, meaning 'an initiate') the search for a personal experience of levels of consciousness, being, or aspects of reality, beyond normal human perception, including communion with a supreme being.

Finding a Path

In their pure form, each of these three methods concentrates on achieving great force of will and strong powers of attention directed to what can simply be called spiritual development or heightened awareness. Each takes many years perhaps decades of intense effort.[69] Each relies on strengthening or perhaps learning to control one part of man's human nature. In the end, each has to give up that path for a time to allow the balanced development of the other faculties, for until all three faculties are functioning harmoniously the imbalance will block further growth. The Yoga would have to learn how to exist in practical world. The monk must adjust to an environment that is not free from emotional distractions. And the person on this path must then use this will power to learn how to balance his emotions and develop his intellect. But they have paid an exceptional price and their further development will benefit from their prior efforts.

Each of these three fundamental approaches also requires a major sacrifice and almost total withdrawal from normal life conditions as the first step. Following

---

[69] St. Theresa of Avila states that it was only after 15 years of cloistered prayer that she even began to have some responses to her prayers.

Finding a Path

any of these approaches would pose an enormous hurdle for most of us and one that is not appropriate for very many as it would not be in keeping with our 'increase and multiply' directive.[70]

The fourth approach, a path in ordinary life is different in many essential ways.[71] It does not demand the major sacrifices of the other approaches be made to begin the path. It makes use of the conditions in life to allow the development of awareness, attention, free will and conscience. It requires work on all three faculties at the same time. It makes no demands for accepting or rejecting a set of beliefs. It relies only on our willingness to observe ourselves uncritically: to learn the truth of ourselves. But what is the truth and how can we approach it: How can we even recognize it? Deep inside ourselves, we may feel the wish to understand.

There are some clues in the Bible. There are over 340 references to man's sleep and the need to awaken. There are over 380 references to man's purpose on earth to seek and to search. And perhaps even more surprising are the

---

[70] Genesis 9:1; 9:7
[71] The term Forth Way was first presented by G. I Gurdjieff.

Finding a Path

almost 2,300 references with the direction to watch and see and an additional 2,200 references to the need to listen. Awakening, searching, seeing and listening are all part of a call to a special kind of vigilance.

From the sheer number of these references we may conclude that Christ's call is for each of us to awaken in order to be able to watch and listen in each moment for what is required of us. Christ gave numerous parables about the need to watch. In Matthew, there is the parable of the five foolish virgins.[72] In Mark the porter is tasked to remain vigilant for the return of the master.[73] In Luke it is the servant that must remain vigilant to guard against the thief.[74] And there are many other biblical directions to watch.

> *...and watching thereunto with all perseverance...*[75]

> *Therefore let us not be asleep like the rest, but awake and sober.*[76]

---

[72] Matthew 25:1-13
[73] Mark 13:34-37
[74] Luke 12:37-39
[75] Ephesians 6:18 KJV
[76] 1 Thessalonians 5:6 NAB

Finding a Path

The ability to hear what is required in this moment and then to be able to do what is required is a mark of a fully developed human with two developed natures. To guide our steps in becoming awake, Christ gave us the path of the Beatitudes.

The task of becoming more vigilant requires a balanced and simultaneous effort of all the faculties of the lower nature; intellect, emotions and body. In looking for a path then, we should consider the possibility of finding a small group of people that also wish to work in this way. The search is made easier if we can find a person who is already working in this way.

And the tests will always be does the group have a goal to awaken in this moment, are all the members able to be sincere in their efforts and observations and perhaps most importantly does participation help me to remember my goal to awaken.

Activities of the group should always serve as a reminder to awaken and not cause one to worry, be concerned or fearful and especially not to analyze or moralize. Christ repeated, many times and in many ways the warning not to judge and our own fall into our

Finding a Path

conditioned response patterns — our waking sleep — is due to our inability and perhaps unwillingness to stop the continual judging. When we are judging we are in a state that is the exact opposite of being awake!

This warning could not be more important and it is the very first and only warning that we know of that was given to Adam and Eve. They were told to stay away from the tree of knowledge of good and evil. Not only do not eat from it but do not even touch the tree.[77]

> *The LORD God gave man this order: "You are free to eat from any of the trees of the garden except the tree of the knowledge of good and bad. From that tree you shall not eat; the moment you eat from it you are surely doomed to die."*[78]

> *... it is only about the fruit of the tree in the middle of the garden that God said, "You shall not eat it or even touch it lest you die."*[79]

---

[77] Genesis 3:3 NAB
[78] Genesis 2:16-17 NAB
[79] Genesis 3:2-13 NAB

Finding a Path

This is a staggering statement of the destructive nature of judging — they should not even touch it. The moment Adam and Eve took that knowledge into themselves — made it a part of their being — they lost their freedom and they began to judge. And yet, despite this biblical injunction we continue to label almost everything as good or evil.

Our path needs to support our efforts to avoid as much as possible this original sin. But avoiding judgment does not free one from acting responsibly in life — living in a way that does not harm others or oneself.

The path we choose must also support Christ's direction to become more vigilant. But what is this vigilance spoken of by Christ? We look and do not see because we do not know how to watch; we hear but do not know how to listen. Our ordinary sight and hearing and other senses are automatically drawn to whatever external or internal event attracts them, often to the exclusion of everything else. We are as passive to these impressions as we are to the associative thoughts and emotions they evoke. This is the way our human nature has been educated. And all thoughts, emotions and movements result from the independent and often unbalanced

Finding a Path

reactions of our intellect, emotions and body to every new impression.

But we will not begin this journey to awaken until we see that we are asleep. The problem is that we have made an assumption based upon our education that our lives are spent in a fully conscious state when this is not the case. Our 'sleep' during our normal waking life is sometimes referred to as waking sleep for in this state we are held spell-bound by whatever external or internal event has attracted our attention. It is what might be called a devilish partnership between our normal intellect and emotions that focuses only on the object or activity and excludes the sensation of ourselves. This waking sleep is called identification.

We will not feel the need to awaken until we become convinced based upon our own experience that our awareness of ourselves [and later in our development our awareness of our connection to higher forces] must be behind all of our actions. Learning how to see becomes the first step toward self-knowledge. This special effort of seeing — this vigilance — will result in a metamorphosis where we begin to love what we see. We will begin to appreciate, to love the act of seeing and

Finding a Path

what is seen. We will delight in the bounty of impressions received anew in each moment. And in time, if we persist we will be made sensitive enough to hear what is required in this moment and in time receive the capability to do what we have heard.

But in the beginning our small attempts to bring an intentional attention into this moment will only verify our inattention. And that is a part of the process we must experience for ourselves. For this to be of value in our development it has to be our personal experience verified countless times until it penetrates the entirety of our being. This is the message of the first two Beatitudes which call us in this moment to see our waking sleep and to see it in all of our daily activities.

The path we choose should support an exploration of how to be awake in the moment. While reading or listening to the experiences of others may be momentarily inspirational such material is of little value if it does not motivate us to seek our own experience of truth just at this moment.

~~~

Finding a Path

An exercise:

If I stop for a moment just now, I can observe that now I am sitting here. I try to notice the sensations arising within me and I become actively aware that I have a body and that I have a presence in this spot. I can take a moment to actually sense, to follow the cycle of my breath, to sense the back of my hands and know without question with this little bit of direct experience I exist; I carry a life energy that I was not aware of before this.

Trying this exercise can make me more vigilant for just a moment. If I can continue this exercise for a bit longer, I see that I can continue to read but that I am simultaneously able to observe sensations arising in myself. And if I can sustain the effort for a short while longer, I may notice that the normal intellectual and emotional chatter subsides. Without "doing" anything but observing myself I was temporarily separated from the control of my lower nature — my identification. This exercise affirms, although only in the smallest way, a higher form of awareness — actually a real self-awareness — that allows the gift of faith to be built in me and begin to feed me with the special energy or grace required to allow my connection to my higher nature.

Finding a Path

~~~

In time the great inflow of grace and energy given during repeated perceptions of truth has the power to erode and replace many fixed ideas and engrained beliefs.

Finding a Path

On Becoming Vigilant

Our great work to be able to become intentional and active participants in the Divine creative process depends on our vigilance. This vigilance, real self-observation, begins with the ability to watch the three lower centers without being diverted — taken — by their automatic reactions. From this state we can begin to see the flow of energies within us. In the beginning the "observer" will be the normal intellect as it is often the only function with an attention that we have a slight ability to control. Later it will take a faculty that can operate at a much higher speed to continue the observations and that faculty lies dormant in the beginning.

With persistence and continued attempts to see, we may in time notice a function that does not fit into the

On Becoming Vigilant

descriptions of the functions found in the faculties of the lower nature. It is a function that had not been noticed before because it lay buried by the automatism of a life lived with only one functioning nature. Beginning to experience this fragile connection to something higher is the opening to our higher nature and the first sign that we may be following the path of the Beatitudes — the path of Christ. It is the first taste of becoming awake.

As we learn to observe our self, our personalities and the activity of the various functions can explain a lot about our normal life and can show how automatically all of our functions operate and how quickly our personalities change. It can also explain how one personality can make commitments that come due when another personality, not in favor of the action, must comply. But from the beginning we have to learn how to avoid categorizing or trying to inventory these observations as that will only turn us back to analysis and moralizing. It is sufficient to know at this point that the newly awakened faculty can record the data … if we can just not judge and analyze.

Observing one's inner activity on multiple occasions and under different conditions in life, we begin to recognize more detail. But until we can see — personally

On Becoming Vigilant

experience in the moment — all of our various functions and personalities and what causes them to arise, we will continue to be automatically taken by them back into our normal stimulus-response existence — our waking sleep. John Newton, Anglican clergyman, poet and lyricist of the hymn "Amazing Grace" wrote in a letter:

> *A real conviction of our weakness we cannot learn merely from books or preachers. The providence of God concurs ... in making us acquainted with ourselves.*[80]

It takes considerable time and effort to be able to catch these parts in the moment: to catch them in the act. If a person only notices certain inner happenings after the fact, the information has already been filtered and altered by one of the lower functions. This after-the-fact review has already rendered the once fresh impression an unreliable form of inner hearsay. And yet we continue to believe these distorted views of ourselves.

One popular aphorism is *carpe diem* [seize the day] and this instinctive urge for a heightened awareness has led

---

[80] Blake, William D. "Almanac of the Christian Church" Minneapolis: Bethany House, 1987

On Becoming Vigilant

many into dangerous, adrenaline-producing pursuits that can give that feeling of being alive in the moment — awake. Activities like drugs, sky-diving, mountain climbing, racing and thrill rides can give moments of heightened awareness but tend to lead one to ever more dangerous pursuits rather than an acquisition of the ability to be open in one's daily life.

There are also many, often expensive, training programs with stated goals to teach people how to live in the present moment originating from the same desire to awaken. But there is no universal method that can work for everyone or even for one person all the time and under different conditions. Each of us approaches this moment of trying with our own unique set of preconditions and personalities. And it would be illogical to assume that the approach that might work for us when we happen to be in an intellectual personality would be appropriate when, moments later we were in an emotionally controlled state. Nor would the method of prayer or meditation in a relaxed and quiet environment necessarily produce beneficial results in the middle of other daily activities. But there are a few clues gleaned from personal experiences of people on the path that can offer help in self-observation.

On Becoming Vigilant

From our own personal experience we know that our emotions and the intellect are time travelers. These two centers spend the majority of their time thinking, wishing and worrying about the future or justifying, fearing, judging and analyzing the past. It is their time travel that is the main cause of the tension, fear and worry that drain the energy that could be used to become open. Their often separate and uncoordinated time travel creates a state of identification where many spend their entire waking lives.

The only faculty that cannot time travel is the physical body which is forever fixed in the present moment. This provides at least a partial clue to how to awaken and stay awake longer. If we can, with appropriate direction, establish a link between our intellect and our body, the intellect can be held in the moment for however briefly the link is maintained. If that connection can be established and strengthened it will in time provide the stable foundation which can gradually constrain the emotional function and bring it into the moment as well. In the beginning, that tenuous link between the body and the intellect is the attention of the intellectual center.

On Becoming Vigilant

When the three centers are present and balanced in the moment, we will have the possibility of being able to connect to that which is higher and in time perhaps opening to a connection with the Divine. Connecting two or more of our normally separate functions may well be the inner meaning of Christ's statement.

> *"For where two or three have gathered together in my name, I am there in their midst."* [81]

For now we will have to see that we live in a state virtually devoid of free will with lives that are habit-driven. All the while we are under the illusion that in this stimulus-response existence we are fully conscious and operating under the power of a free will. In the Bible there are hundreds of calls for us to awaken from this dream-like existence — our waking sleep.

Christ's message is repeated in many different ways in the New Testament but the call is always to be vigilant. [82]

---

[81] Matthew 18:20 NASB
[82] Matthew 25:1-13 ; Mark 13:32-37 ; Matthew 26:38-41 ; Luke 12:37-39 ; Revelation 3:2-4

On Becoming Vigilant

To be vigilant in this way means that we have to cultivate an inner space or faculty where silence prevails and we can be non-attached to the illusions that continue to arise from the mechanical parts of our lower nature. These illusions that we cling to so tenaciously, continue to mask the reality we need to see. We wish to know what is true in this moment — our reality. And like the watchman standing guard at night, we have to accept to look into the darkness — accept the darkness — accept the silence: in some cases for long periods without seeing or hearing anything. To be able do this we must acquire a vigilance that is strong enough to ignore the pressure of the lower nature to fill this void with mental or physical activity and more illusions. We do not see that we cling to these illusions with a clinched fist resisting our possible freedom. But as many have said down through history, to be free to receive, to be open to the gift of grace we must approach the unknown with an empty hand. The practice of praying with arms outstretched and palms raised can be a reminder of this essential need to become internally open and receptive.

Real vigilance will call relaxation and the opening to the impressions we must have to feed our higher nature. And as long as we are tense, we will know and we will

On Becoming Vigilant

feel our refusal to accept this gift of opening to a divine presence. If we can be vigilant in this way, we may see that on occasion we will become less attached to outer events and the inner activity our normal intellect and emotions and we will sense a new freedom — freedom to see what is here for us — now.

Vigilance to this degree may be considered the highest form of prayer or meditation: prayer without words: a quality of being rather than a formatted recital. This prayerful state can and should be our goal at every moment in our daily life.

To attain this prayerful state, this state of presence in the middle of our busy day is the preparation required to be able to hear and do the tasks we have been placed on earth to accomplish.

The First Beatitude — Coming Back to the Present

Again we see that we have lost contact with ourselves and slipped back into our normal state completely unaware of the loss of the connection to something higher which might have been experienced in the earlier exercise. We can however, use that realization as a reminder to again make an effort to return to the present.

~~~

An exercise:

I adjust my posture so that it is more erect and put my feet on the floor. I place my attention on sensations arising in my feet. If I am able to continue this simple

The First Beatitude – Coming Back to the Present

effort, I may notice that something inside begins to grow calm. Even though I am only making a small effort to be aware of the impressions coming from my feet, an intentional effort called sensing, I notice that after a time the awareness seems to spread of its own — without my effort — to include more of my body.

~~~

This simple exercise is one method by which a person may begin to awaken in order to be able to follow the path of the Beatitudes.

> *Blessed are the poor in spirit, for theirs is the kingdom of heaven*[83]

In being reminded that we were not awake just before we started the exercise, we can understand in a very small way the first part of the first Beatitude — we are poor in spirit. We were, just before the small effort, asleep, living in only a small part of ourselves. But in making the effort to awaken, we see that our small effort seems to be augmented by a larger awareness that is not from us. We can on occasion experience the second part

---

[83] Matthew 5:3 KJV

The First Beatitude – Coming Back to the Present

of the first Beatitude, *'for theirs is the kingdom of heaven'* but the experience is fragile and easily lost. This gift of another form of awareness that we cannot properly claim is of our doing is an exact verification in one's own experience of the statement that to those who have much, more will be given.[84]

We cannot maintain this effort for long for we lack the energy to maintain our attention and we will simply fall victim to distractions taking us back into our normal waking sleep subject to external events and internal habits. This is lawful and like night follows day another manifestation of natural laws. But we can to try again.

In time we may begin to understand why prayers are not answered and special practices do not produce lasting effect. As we are, we cannot stay awake long enough to ask much less to hear a response. We are not real, fully realized humans functioning with both of our natures.

> *But let him ask in faith, nothing wavering. For he that wavereth is like a wave of the sea driven with the wind and tossed. For let not that man think that he shall receive any thing*

---

[84] Matthew 13:12, 25:29; Mark 4:24; Luke 12:48

The First Beatitude – Coming Back to the Present

> *of the Lord. A double-minded man is unstable in all his ways.*[85]

We are not open no matter how much we might think we are and it is even the conviction that we are open and unbiased that hypnotizes us in our waking sleep. And in some cases, our prayers recalled from memory and recited by our normal intellect perhaps even with a bit of emotion drown out the opportunity to hear a response or to discern God's message for us.

In a moment of acknowledging this inability to hear the call and not even knowing how to listen, we see that our human nature has been totally in control — we are missing a connection to [are poor in] our spiritual nature. We will see with our own experience that we lack the energy, the attention and will power to maintain this first small step for even a few moments in the middle of our daily existence. But the value of this first step cannot be overstated. Its ability to allow us to break for even a moment the momentum of our ordinary lives is substantial. But many stop here.

---

[85] James 1:6-8 KJV

The First Beatitude – Coming Back to the Present

> *With a false modesty, people rest content with partial and provisional truths, no longer seeking to ask radical questions about the meaning and ultimate foundation of human, personal and social existence.*[86]

To go further requires that we increase the frequency and duration of these special moments of heightened awareness. We must try to be watchful while the entire set of experience and knowledge accumulated over our lifetime by the lower nature has been constructed to keep us asleep. It is as Michel Conge says the greatest of all games: a real life-or-death struggle. We are playing this game against our lower nature — ourselves. His lower nature he calls Doctor Conge and he is a full tenured Professor specializing in his inner life.

> *You have to outwit him, be stronger, more intelligent than he is. Just imagine, he holds all the cards, and you have to win! He's been dealt both hands, his and yours.*[87]

---

[86] John Paul II, "Fides et Ratio [Faith and Reason]" Encyclical Letter To The Bishops of the Catholic Church on the Relationship between Faith and Reason. Pg.4

[87] Conge, Michel, *Inner Octaves,* Dolmen Meadows Edition, Toronto, 2007, pp. 117-119

The First Beatitude – Coming Back to the Present

~~~

Before passing on to the discussion of the second Beatitude it might be useful to mention that throughout the Old Testament there are many references to "fear of the Lord" as a first step in spiritual development. This is not the servile fear of being robbed or being in a car accident. Rather this fear is more like awe and honor given by a disciple to his teacher in recognition of the imperfect state of the student. It includes the concept of desire to learn.

We are given moments when we are placed in a situation for which there is no automatic answer or action. Just in these very short moments, before our habits regain control, we get a taste of our limitations and on occasion of a vast unknown in which our ordinary impressions seem to become greatly enhanced and the perception of time seems to slow. This glimpse can be unsettling and our ordinary minds try to arrange our lives to prevent their occurance or define them away with some logical sounding explanation. But these special moments, devoid of names or rational explanations are only a small foretaste of what St. John of the Cross called the dark

The First Beatitude – Coming Back to the Present

night of the soul[88] in which all of our knowledge and experience drops away in the face of a greater although unknown truth. These moments can produce a certain kind of fear of the unknown which can be a precursor of "fear of the Lord."

The following excepts from Proverbs support the idea that this is the step identified in the first Beatitude.

> *The fear of the LORD is the beginning of wisdom,*[89]
>
> *The fear of the LORD is the instruction for wisdom,*[90]
>
> *Then you will discern the fear of the LORD And discover the knowledge of God.*[91]

And while the concept of "fear of the Lord" has passed out of common use replaced by Christ's image and teaching of love, there is a lawful amount of anxiety that can arise when seeing how far we are from what we could be. Hopefully that anxiety can produce [or call] the energy or grace to strive to become vigilant.

---

[88] St. John of the Cross, "Dark Night of the Soul" Dover Publications, Inc. 2003
[89] Proverbs 9:10
[90] Proverbs 15:33
[91] Proverbs 2:5

The First Beatitude – Coming Back to the Present

Sri Ramakrishna, (1836 –1886) a famous mystic of 19th-century India, said

> *People weep rivers of tears because a son is not born or because they cannot get riches. But who sheds even one teardrop because he has not seen God?* [92]

The call is to recognize and reclaim our birthright and for this the parable of the prodigal son perfectly illustrates what is required.[93] Like the prodigal son, we have been given our inheritance but spend most of our days caught by the web of our activity and separated even from the remembrance of God or of our desire to awaken. But like the prodigal son we may in time, thru the mercy of God, be brought to see that something essential is missing in us that is only available from above. Our goal then is at all costs to become open to receive what already is prepared for those who can accept. This is the message of Christ and the reason he prepared and opened a path for us. But it will always remain a

---

[92] Swami Prabhavananda, "The Sermon on the Mount According to Vedanta" A Mentor Book, New American Library, New York, pg. 20.
[93] Luke 15: 11-32

The First Beatitude – Coming Back to the Present

path that we must be willing to follow on our own. This path requires that we be willing to accept our partial development and the lack of connection to that which is higher in ourselves and beyond.

The Beatitudes call for a new beginning — a liberation from all that has kept us in a state of conditioned habitual behavior. Those who have made and continue to make the effort to try and awaken can be truly called Blessed for they have been granted the grace, the energy, the wish to begin Christ's journey.

The First Beatitude – Coming Back to the Present

The Second Beatitude — Seeing One's Condition

Blessed are they that mourn, for they shall be comforted[94]

Even though the efforts to wake up in the first Beatitude can produce profound changes in our state — our level of being — for brief moments, it is only a foretaste of what awaits. Much is still required of us. The second Beatitude marks the beginning of self-observation and the test of our willingness to pay for what awaits. If we continue to try and awaken, after a time we may notice that reminders to try and come back [awaken] are coming more frequently as they will in proportion to our efforts.

---

[94] Matthew 5:4 KJV

The Second Beatitude – Seeing One's condition

It is interesting to see that caught in the middle of life, trapped in the momentum of our day and deep in our habitual state of waking-sleep somehow a reminder is noticed. We have been "asleep at the wheel" but something new reminds us, calls us to try anew. In part this gift or reminder is given in proportion to our repeated small efforts. With each effort to come back into the moment, small memories are created in all three centers simultaneously. If repeated under the same conditions, say just before breakfast, we may begin to sense reminders to awake not only then but also potentially at other meals or perhaps whenever seated in the same chair. But these are only reminders and only have value if we use them to try and come back to a sense of ourselves — awaken.

Our internal lives are spent as if we were lost and walking around in a darkened city. Each moment of awareness has the same effect as turning on one small street light. Not very much light in a big city but at least one spot where, should we pass again, we can pause and know that we are here just at this moment. The goal is to turn on all the lights in this inner city of twisting avenues and dangerous personalities.

The Second Beatitude – Seeing One's condition

Each moment of awareness opens us to a flow of new grace which we may sense as renewed energy: Energy that can enliven and feed our higher functions: the energy that is contained in unfiltered impressions.

The first function that is awakened is the one that can act as the impartial observer. Because it can only function with the finer energy produced in moments of awareness it will, for a time, be very weak and easily overpowered by our automatic conditioned responses. This observer must become more present in our lives as it alone has the speed and capability to build the solid foundation of truth required to follow the path of the Beatitudes.

In the beginning, the function of the observer must be handled by an intermediary function. And for a time, all that we will be able to do is distinguish ourselves from what we recognize as our normal "I." We will see that we are not our normal thoughts, feelings, sensations and associations which have little unity or energy. But these observations with our limited attention begin to allow the whole of ourselves to be brought into a more appropriate state and the normally dissipated energy wasted on unnecessary tension to be conserved for ourselves. In a balanced state the body will be able to

The Second Beatitude – Seeing One's condition

manufacture and move the food necessary for the awakening of the observer: but only so long as we can maintain this state.

With sufficient time and effort, this new observer will become the seat of real emotions capable of receiving the divine gifts of faith, hope and love. Unlike our normal emotions habituated in our lower nature, it has no negative part. It serves the function of providing a repository for understanding acquired from real personal experience — unfiltered observations. These perceptions are blocked for now by what we think and feel we know already. But rightly conducted observations of self in many circumstances will begin to erode that misconception and many other unsupported facts. Later, in the fourth stage, we will have been made able to absorb the perceptions of reality — righteousness — and that will provide us with an even stronger feel for truth.

This higher function which we hope to have awakened in us and which can provide the "feel for truth" or we might say lead us in righteousness is called conscience. It is separate from and of a much higher order than the morality one has been taught to follow as a child.

The Second Beatitude – Seeing One's condition

The morality of our childhood resides in memory and habits of the lower nature. Until our higher nature can begin to function, the dictates of the moral code we have been taught can provide useful boundaries for right action, for that support and guidance may even help to remind us to awaken and protect us until we have completed the path of the Beatitudes. A fully functioning conscience will in time provide a counterbalance to a more rigid — habit driven — observance of "morality" with the result that virtuous actions will be motivated by understanding and wisdom and not fear or habits.

The French mystic Marguerite Porete went so far as to say that for the conscious being, or as she says, the simple soul united with God there is nothing required but God's love. Her writings and those of her contemporary, Meister Eckhart, state that the soul is

> ... *above the demands of ordinary virtue, not because virtue is not needed but because in its state of union with God virtue becomes automatic.*[95]

---

[95] Porete, Marguerite "The Mirror of Simple Souls," http://en.wikipedia.org/wiki/Marguerite_Porete

The Second Beatitude – Seeing One's condition

A short time later after Porete published her writing in 1380, an anonymous monk speaks directly to the need to develop this connection to real conscience, a real connection to God's divine love, wisdom, input of the Holy Spirit or however you might choose to define it.

> *Only the prayer love from your heart can penetrate the cloud of unknowing. Don't give up. If any thoughts arise in your mind – no matter how holy – ignore them. And ignore feelings of bliss and visions and miracles. Focus on his love and his relationship with you.*[96]

This prayer probably predates Christianity, and is found in every major religion. In the 1960's, the prayer was repackaged by three Catholic priests and renamed Centering Prayer.

However, reaching this stage takes a significant amount of self-observation. Again the old adages apply:

> *... the truth shall set you free*[97];

---

[96] Anonymous, "The Cloud Of Unknowing" 1380,
[97] John 8:32

The Second Beatitude – Seeing One's condition

Know thyself.[98]

And this is the call in the second Beatitude: to become ever more vigilant — to see more and more of oneself under varied conditions.

Our efforts to learn how to observe and listen attentively are our payment. It is interesting that one of the original definitions of suffering contained the idea of payment for something desired. And it is exactly this *suffering* that is described in the second Beatitude. A significant part of the *suffering* will result from the efforts to distance ourselves from what we consider "our" thoughts. Now we are a victim of our thoughts because we do not know that it is possible to disassociate ourselves from them. And we have yet to experience how large an obstacle they are to our awakening. Our thoughts automatically name everything that enters our awareness. And the use of the pronoun "I" as if we were a singular being while in every different personality is one of the greatest obstacles to self-awareness, spiritual growth and consciousness.

---

[98] From Greek mythology this was carved into the temple of the Oracle at Delphi.

The Second Beatitude – Seeing One's condition

As we continue to try to awaken and stay awake longer we should strive to avoid naming and analyzing everything observed. It will become increasingly clear how seldom we remember this, how easily we are taken by every thought and emotion, how quickly our lower nature names what we are seeing and how difficult it is to stay present for even a short period.

However, at what appears to be the same moment that we observe ourselves taken by automatic thoughts, feelings and actions we may feel what might be called a small "jolt." This small and often short duration jab is called remorse of conscience — *re~morse*, a bite again. It is the result of a new impression confronting our previously stored and automatically recalled names, opinions and beliefs — memories. Unfortunately in the beginning because we do not as yet have the strength of attention or will power to remain awake, the lower nature and its mechanical responses quickly move in to make moral assessments, dismiss, analyze or justify.

We have been educated and habitualized — taught — to judge and name everything. And these habits made by our automatic parts are based upon processes and procedures, definitions and descriptions provided by

The Second Beatitude – Seeing One's condition

family, educators, friends and societal values developed and accepted by others over centuries. And although they may have originated from Christ or other saints or enlightened people, they have been passed down through generations of people who like our self are rarely awake. Over time the essence of the truth behind the teaching becomes layered beneath rigid interpretations and forms. These fixed ideas and attitudes become the strongest part of the chains that bind us in our lower nature. We have been educated that they are good and necessary and do not want to let go of them. It is this belief supported by our ego and its two allies: vanity and pride that sucks the vitality and value from each new impression.

Christ gives us the requirement for this stage by repeating over and over the warning not to judge for it is our set of fixed ideas, opinions, and rigid codes of conduct that must be abandoned. But it is much too early in one's journey for us to have the experience, strength of attention and force of will necessary for so great a change. But we can rest assured that in time, if we persist, our conscience will be developed to the point that this new freedom can emerge as another gift from above.

The Second Beatitude – Seeing One's condition

While some may have less difficulty accepting to see the moment of remorse for what it is, a reminder of one's sleep and an opportunity to try and come back to one's self — to awaken — others may find this stage particularly challenging. This is especially true for those who have been taught to feel guilty — and blame themselves out of habit. The truth is that when we are in a state of waking sleep, controlled by ego and habits, our will is not free and we are simple acting as stimulus-response organisms like other animals. And worse yet, we are reacting with this habit given to us by others. For just like Adam and Eve we had to be taught how to feel guilty. Perhaps Rumi says it more simply.

> *Why should we grieve that we've been sleeping?*
> *It doesn't matter how long we've been unconscious*
> *We're groggy, but let the guilt go.*
> *Feel the motion of tenderness*
> *Around you, the buoyancy*[99]

Just in this moment we may see that we have fallen back to sleep and we can try again to awaken and move though the first stage of accepting that we were lost in

---

[99] Rumi, "Buoyancy" extract - Barks, Coleman translator, *The Essential Rumi*, Harper One, 2004, pg 105

The Second Beatitude – Seeing One's condition

our normal associations and in time we may be able to stay awake long enough to move back into the second stage. As we persist in our self-observation we will *suffer* more — mourn. We will have to continue to pay over and over for the gifts we have been given and the even greater gifts we wish to receive. We must become much more vigilant.

One question that will inevitably arise is how long must we stay in this stage. St. Theresa of Avila, living in a cloister with few of our normal distractions and with many periods of the day devoted to prayer, states that it was fifteen years before she began to receive responses to her prayers. St. Theresa calls the later stages of the second Beatitude the Period of Quiet when nothing we do makes any discernible change in our condition.[100] She states that most novices leave the convent and lay people switch to another religion, practice or church, fall back on habitual practices or simply turn away because they do not understand the need for extensive self-observation. We will stay in this stage, falling asleep and then awakening to observe until we have been brought

---

[100] St. Teresa of Avila, "The Interior Castle" translated and edited by E. Allison Peers, Image Books, Garden City New York, 1961

The Second Beatitude – Seeing One's condition

to accept on a deep organic level our inability to remain present with our own effort. It is not given to us to know when this gift of opening will be granted and until then we must continue to "pay" with our efforts to be ever more vigilant — present.

It is interesting that in the Catholic Church the sacrament of penance is provided to encourage a person to look inward and observe more of their actions in every situation. Preparation for this sacrament was called an examination of conscience, for it is the conscience, that faculty of our higher nature that can perceive the truth of our actions. And because having a connection to one's conscience was already a mark of a person on the path of the Beatitudes it was held in high regard. If this part is skipped or if a person does not have a developing conscience, the Catholic sacrament becomes simply an admission of guilt for violating a moral code and an acceptance of some penance or repayment to negate its effects. That sacrament of penance with its removal of guilt is of great value, but much more is lost.

In Judaism, this task of self-observation is given a preeminent part on their religious calendar. New Year's Day in the Jewish calendar [Rosh Hashanah] begins the

The Second Beatitude – Seeing One's condition

ten High Holy Days and culminates in the Day of Atonement (Yom Kippur). The Hebrew month preceding Rosh Hashanah, Elul, is designated as a month of introspection and repentance. During this period, Jews are instructed to begin a process of intense self-examination and repentance. Repentance [Teshuvah] or returning -- involves a threefold process: reaching inward (examining oneself and one's life); reaching upward (seeking a meaningful relationship with God, the source of all life); and reaching outward (rededicating oneself to the service of others). Add to this the requirement to be present to these actions as they occur rather than simply remembering them after the filters of the lower nature have stored the distorted memories.

In both religions, the true significance of this task of self-observation is shown by the central role assigned to these services.

But the examination of conscience for a person on the path of the Beatitudes is not a look back to past actions which have been filtered and distorted thru the mechanical analysis of the lower faculties but a look now at the truth of this moment.

The Second Beatitude – Seeing One's condition

The second part of this Beatitude states that those who persist will be given the comfort [grace; energy] to endure what is being seen.

> *It is especially in the beginning of conversion that he anoints the ulcers with the oil of His pity lest a man should be more aware than is desirable of the extent of his disease and the difficulty of the cure.*[101]

---

[101] St. Bernard as quoted in Wu, Obl. O.S.B., J.D., John C. H. "The Interior Carmel: The Threefold Way Of Love" Sheen & Ward, New York, 1953, pg. 104

A Short Note on Self-Observation

It is natural that as we try to observe ourselves we will occasionally experience a newfound energy enlivening our being. Often what appears to be new-found energy is simply the result of reducing the energy lost from unnecessary tension arising in our waking sleep from our automatic functions. But in time we may also begin to produce and receive additional energy of a much higher and finer quality. This energy at times can become so intense that it cannot be contained without damage to the body. The body's normal mechanism for eliminating this kind of excess energy is thru talking. But on occasion the energy overwhelms our system and we will experience unexplained crying, laughing, or fidgeting.

A Short Note on Self-Observation

Examples of this abound. For when we are placed in a life threatening situation we are forcibly awakened by our instinctive functions. In this heightened state of awareness the body produces very fine chemicals that allow us to escape the conditions or react appropriately. Once the dangerous conditions are removed many will find themselves laughing, shaking, or crying uncontrollably as the body begins to remove or neutralize the chemicals like adrenaline that have been produced for our protection.

Fortunately our early experiences of trying to remain awake do not produce large amounts of these chemicals — this energy — and the elimination process often is completed thru minor fidgeting and excessive talking. We must be careful however and try to eliminate this excess energy appropriately. Often people eliminate the excess energy from the new observations by trying to tell people what they have seen, or share with them some new discovery when the person they are talking to is not interested. Even when motivated by a sincere desire to share, this action may cause problems in our ordinary lives. And if we keep going over the experience with our ordinary mind [inner talking of the lower intellect] we

A Short Note on Self-Observation

could also create obstacles when the ego mimics what has been seen. For that reason Christ gave a warning.

> *Give not that which is holy unto the dogs, neither cast ye your pearls before swine, lest they trample them under their feet, and turn again and rend you.*[102]

Our ego, vanity and pride as manifest in each of our separate personalities are one way of interpreting "swine" And we have already seen how the faculties of our lower nature take each new impression and strip away its freshness and vitality and in the process, drag us back into sleep.

For that reason it is valuable to gather a small group of similarly striving people. Then with the aid of a guide, the members of the group can all try the same exercise. Gathering back together, each person's observations can serve to eliminate their excess energy and at the same time enlarge the experience for the others. This can add new perspectives to our own observations and our observations provide the opportunity in a safe

---

[102] Matthew 7:6

A Short Note on Self-Observation

environment to eliminate the waste products of the impressions we received.

The Third Beatitude — A Gift

Blessed are the meek for they shall inherit the earth.[103]

Many words have been written and spoken about the meaning of meek. The root of the word meek comes from the early Middle English word *miúkr, mjúkr* meaning soft, pliant, gentle and free from self-will.[104] This and other more contemporary definitions have only served to start almost as many arguments and discussions about the meaning of the word meek as there have been discussions about the type of fish that must have swallowed Jonah — and most to the same benefit.

---

[103] Matthew 5:5 KJV
[104] "The Shorter Oxford English Dictionary" by William Little *etal* Claredon Press, Oxford 1978. *Vol. II; pg. 1301*

The Third Beatitude – A Gift

Gerald Heard suggests that the Greek testament word *praos* [πραος] or meek was applied to wild animals that had been tamed to work with men.[105] The word was also applied to strong and powerful domestic animals like horses or oxen also trained to be of use to a human. In this sense those who have been made meek are those whose powerful and automatic impulses [parts of the human nature: ego, vanity, pride, ordinary learned emotions and thoughts] have been put into intentional and understanding service of a higher force. With this definition we can see how such strong and forceful beings as Moses and Paul the apostle could be called meek.

To allow ourselves to be made meek is not an easy task and can take years. It is not so hard to accept that actions we have been taught are "bad" in ourselves should be tamed but experience will show that the much tougher habits to control are the ones we really like and perhaps tougher still are the ones we have been taught to defend as "good." In fact we are often not quite ready to even give up some of our "not-so-good" habits and a quote

---

[105] Heard, Gerald, "The Code of Christ" Harper and Brothers Publishers, New York, 1942 pp. 63-64

The Third Beatitude – A Gift

both humorous and exquisitely true from St. Augustine illustrates our condition.

> ... *when I prayed you for chastity and said: 'Grant me chastity and continence, but not yet.' I was afraid you might hear my prayer quickly, and that you might too rapidly heal me...*[106]

We are exactly like that. We see that we are ready to get rid of the "bad" in our self as long as we get to keep the pleasurable and continue the "good" habits. But the challenge is to give up our attachment to all of our fixed ideas, knowledge, certainty, feelings, habits and beliefs in order to be made able to accept God's direction.

> *In my search to see reality in myself, I may come to the door of perception. But it will not open, truth will not be revealed, so long as I cling to what I know. I need to have empty hands to approach the unknown.*[107]

---

[106] Augustine, Saint, "Confession" Oxford University Press, 1998, pg. 145

[107] Jeanne de Salzmann, "The Reality of Being" Shambhala Publications, Inc. Boston and London, 2010

The Third Beatitude – A Gift

This clearly is an enormous task and one that cannot happen without a lot of time, effort, external support and guidance. And despite the realization that these barriers to growth must be removed, we will see that we do not know how to accomplish this. And there will be many suggestions made by our lower nature and ego from existing knowledge … the parts that should be ignored.

Although the first two Beatitudes have been preparing us to be "meeked," the third Beatitude marks a deep acceptance that we cannot advance our ability to stay awake to our connection to our higher faculties. We will have had to start over at the first Beatitude and accept that no matter how many times we have tried, we were again, just before this moment of being reminded, asleep. And with extended periods of self-observation in the second stage — the second Beatitude — we will have been given unequivocal evidence — the real truth of our existence — that we are powerless against our habits and the control of our ego, vanity and pride.

If and when this truth is finally accepted, organically, with the whole of our being, we will be willing to set aside "our ideas" and accept guidance: a willingness to be taught. And in addition, we will have been given the

The Third Beatitude – A Gift

beginning of a sincere wish to learn God's individual and unique plan for each of us.

This final stage in becoming meek is illustrated in the words of the apostles as they sought to spread the message of Christ. Despite their best efforts in seeking converts in Asia to the teachings of Christ, they were meeting with no success. Their experience was that using their best efforts — relying on their own knowledge and beliefs — they were incapable of reaching their goal of spreading Christ's message of love and hope.

> *... we were crushed beyond our strength, even to despairing of life. We were left to feel like men condemned to death so that we might trust, not in ourselves, but in God ...*[108]

In this moment of truth they sensed with all of their being that "they" could not accomplish their mission.[109] Here again we see the nature of the path at this critical stage between the second and third Beatitude: vigilance and persistence in our efforts to observe ourselves.

---

[108] 2 Corinthians 1 : 8-10 NAB
[109] Luke 15: 11-32. The prodigal son parable is another example of this "death and rebirth" stage in Spiritual growth.

The Third Beatitude – A Gift

Unless you are lucky enough to get struck down off your horse like Paul on the road to Damascus[110], the path of the Beatitudes indicates that like the quote from the Apostles, we will have to continue to strive until we have been sufficiently prepared.

After the apostle's deep realization where in a moment their ego was subdued, they could begin to understand Christ's statement.

> *My grace is enough for you, for in weakness power reaches perfection.*[111]

After that the apostles continued to preach and the number of converts to Christianity multiplied as did their faith.

The poetry of Rumi supports the universality of the steps along the path of the Beatitudes in different cultures and religions. It recognizes this critical stage in spiritual development where we sense with the whole of our being our inability to make ourselves suitable for salvation or heaven through our own efforts.

---

[110] Acts 9:1-19
[111] 2 Corinthians 12 : 9 NAB

The Third Beatitude – A Gift

I didn't come here of my own accord, and I can't leave that way.

Whoever brought me here, will have to take me home.[112]

After moving up and down countless times through the stages of awakening and self-observation we may be made meek — opened. And in the moment that we become open so many more new and valuable impressions rush in and provide food for our higher functions. This inrush of new impressions and energy which St. Theresa of Avila likened to a stream of fresh water entering the garden which before that had required our efforts to carry buckets of water from afar. This new and freely flowing source of grace can at times provide so much energy that the body cannot contain it. But as stated earlier, the body has automatic, instinctive methods to eliminate excess energy.

The Earth — What a gift! The reward of the third Beatitude could not be more precise. In moments we will be reminded to awaken, allowed to come back into our

---

[112] Rumi, "Who Says Words With My Mouth?" Barks, Coleman translator, *The Essential Rumi*, Harper One, 2004, pg 2

The Third Beatitude – A Gift

selves loosening the bonds of the habitual. And then, if we have the energy to continue, our inner chaos will be quietened and we may be given a clear view of a world freed from words and automatic associations. The brave new world that opens for us contains many experiences and impressions that can feed our higher centers and enliven our developing conscience.

In exchange we also begin to acquire responsibilities to both the source of our gifts and the earth we inhabit. In a very real way we must now strive to become intentional channels of the creative energy flowing down from above and the re-creative energy that can flow through us to higher levels as we ingest new impression. In this process, which until now has occurred through us as passive participants due to our one natured being, we become an intentional contributor in the universal ecology of reciprocal feeding and care where life at all levels is interdependent. Of course our responsibilities at this stage are few because we are still far from being able to remain awake long enough to accomplish any but the smallest tasks and our ability to know what could help is undeveloped.

The Third Beatitude – A Gift

And it will be abundantly clear that we did not reach this stage by ourselves for we are still too easily caught by the activities of life and our own conditioned reflexes and continually fall asleep in our habits. Over and over we must strive to regain this stage, falling asleep and trying again to awaken. But now having been given a taste of our rightful inheritance we must continue to play a more active role in the maintenance of this great gift.

The Third Beatitude – A Gift

The Fourth Beatitude — Gathering Truth

Blessed are they that hunger and thirst for righteousness, for they shall be filled[113]

Having received the gift of the earth in moments we are awake, we will have traveled many times up and down the path of the first triad of the Beatitudes: Seeing that we have been asleep, moments of self-observation, becoming meek and then back into waking sleep. The second triad begins like the first with the task to see; to learn. This again is a renewed call to vigilance but having been made more porous and open [meek], we become like a sponge soaking up new impressions. We have been given a real hunger for the truth of our

---

[113] Matthew 5:6 KJV

The Fourth Beatitude – Gathering Truth

existence and a renewed desire to search for a way to escape the control of our lower nature.

> *For the Son of Man is as a man taking a far journey, who left his house, ... and commanded the porter to watch. ... Lest coming suddenly he find you sleeping ... And what I say unto you I say unto all, watch.*[114]

As with the porter, our vigilance must extend to anything and everything. Impressions intentionally accepted and not pirated by the lower nature, feed the higher faculties which in turn strengthen our wish. Nothing is trivial or unimportant for that is just another mechanical response of the intellect and the work of the ego to put us back to sleep.

> *People do not pour new wine into old wineskins. If they do, the skins burst, the wine spills out, and the skins are ruined.* [115]

The old wineskins are our ordinary mind's set of knowledge, values and morality that reside in our lower nature. And like most of our fixed ideas and values they

---

[114] Mark 13:33-37 KJV
[115] Matthew 9:17 NAB; Mark 2:22; Luke 5:37

The Fourth Beatitude – Gathering Truth

are for the most part rigid and inflexible and cannot be stretched to accept the new truths being seen. The new impressions of ourselves and the external world observed in moments of presence are full of a very fine energy. And in the same way our lower nature processes physical foods, these impressions will undergo a natural "fermentation" or digestion as they are processed by our higher nature. And exactly like the processes for physical food a part will go for our own growth, a part will serve higher purposes and some part will have to be eliminated. This process of digestion is not compatible with the faculties of the lower nature and cannot be contained by their rigid habits and fixed ideas. But more importantly, when we are in our one-natured, waking sleep, the faculties of the lower nature stand absolutely in the way of this essential operation of digestion.

> *If you seek perfection, go, sell your possessions and give to the poor. You will then have treasure in heaven. Afterward, come back and follow me. Hearing these words, the young man went away sad, for his possessions were many.*[116]

---

[116] Matthew 19: 21-22: Mark 10: 21-23: Luke 18: 22-25

The Fourth Beatitude – Gathering Truth

"If you seek perfection" presents an interesting challenge in the modern age of Christianity where many are relying on the phrase that 'God accepts you just as you are.' And while it is the true that God does understand our situation and patiently awaits our return, it does not mean we have been given a free pass into heaven. And the problem with this common phrase is that it does not necessarily motivate one to search — to become like the teacher. It can have the opposite effect and put one solidly to sleep with the hypnotic idea that everything will be OK — nothing is required.

But although perfection seems far from possible it is only because we do not understand what perfection could mean in our lives and we cannot see how we can do it. And so we are unwilling to let go of our fixed ideas because we do not have the faith to become open and allow the process to be fulfilled in us: The faith that we need is the faith that can move the internal "mountain" of fixed habits and ideas that are blocking our path back to God.[117] But a quote from a different tradition by Swami Prabhavananda may give a bit more insight into the requirement.

---

[117] Matthew 17:20

The Fourth Beatitude – Gathering Truth

> *"In our ignorance it is hard for us to believe that God can be realized. ... Hindu call this state samadi; Buddhists call it nirvana; Christians call it the mystical union, or union with God. ... Most people argue whether one can find God, or whether perfection can be achieved or not, or what Christ meant by knowing the truth or seeing God. ... How can a spiritual aspirant who is longing for the truth be satisfied with theology, with philosophy, with doctrines and creeds? Sri Ramakrishna used to tell the devotees: 'You have come to the mango garden. What good is it to count the leaves on the trees? Eat the mangoes and satisfy your hunger!'"* [118]

Questions will arise and they are a sign that we have accepted that we do not know. Questions work to weaken our ego, vanity and pride for they are an acceptance of the truth that we do not know. And from this questioning, a deep longing begins to emerge. This longing, this hunger from deep within a more real part of ourselves is a real prayer — a prayer that will not be denied. That is the message of the fourth Beatitude.

---

[118] Swami Prabhavananda, "The Sermon on the Mount according to Vedanta" New American Library, A Mentor Book, New York, July, 1972, pp. 69 ff.

The Fourth Beatitude – Gathering Truth

~~~

An exercise:

Remembering to keep a part of our attention on the impressions coming into and arising from within the body [an intentional act of sensing] can help us stay awake in our daily activities. Such intentional sensing need only be focused on a small part of the body. It could be any part of the body. As an example, in the morning we could choose to make a sincere effort each time we remember, to maintain a part of our attention on our face allowing the muscles of the face to relax while we are talking to others. This can allow us to actively listen instead of letting the normal associative mind wait for an opening to inject our experience or view.

The exercise should be changed periodically, for natural forces available to the lower nature will make it difficult to remember after a week or so of trying. In addition our egoism will soon start commenting that we are not getting anything from this exercise so why continue to make the same efforts. And one cannot expect to always be able to free oneself from the attractions of life that put us to sleep. But it does not matter if we cannot get to a

The Fourth Beatitude – Gathering Truth

more focused state — it is the effort that is essential. But if we sincerely wish to see the truth of ourselves, we must also see, experience for ourselves, how an effort that starts intentionally can be quickly neutralized or perhaps even worse, automatized by the lower nature to the point that we are led to believe we are making efforts when we are only thinking about the effort.

~~~

So far in this journey of the Beatitudes, we have been instructed to prepare to sacrifice all we ordinarily believe to be true and become more watchful. We must strive to be watchful while the entire set of experiences and knowledge accumulated over our lifetime by the lower nature has been constructed to keep us asleep.

Our attempts to be vigilant have to be intensified, varied, and applied in different life situations using different approaches. But the fundamental requirement must remain: all efforts must to be intentional as the work to which we have been called to can never become habitual. We may also notice that to the measure that we can make intentional efforts, we will also be given more reminders.

The Fourth Beatitude – Gathering Truth

It is evidence that we are being called: we are being given the energy [grace] to increase our efforts.

In moments of presence we are given a taste of pure, unfiltered truth and to the degree that we have valued it like the pearl of great price, our wish for more can grow. This is the state of the fourth Beatitude.

> *Blessed are they that hunger and thirst for righteousness, for they shall be filled*[119]

The reward for our small efforts to be vigilant is staggering. Most people fail to appreciate that truth has a real beauty and a certain materiality. It is a form of energy and energy and matter differ only in relative fineness. Science is only recently beginning to equate energy with information, we might say truth. This means that the reward for vigilance is an inflow of energy and more truth. This energy, if not taken by the lower nature, feeds our spiritual development through the growth of our conscience, our consciousness, our soul and ultimately begins, if only in a very small way, to repay our Creator's endless gifts.

---

[119] Matthew 5:6

The Fourth Beatitude – Gathering Truth

Like the parable of the talents[120] we have been given the responsibility to make ourselves available for the gift of this growth. If we do not, we may be like the servant in this parable that hid the money [talents] he was given and was *"cast … into outer darkness"* where *"… there shall be weeping and gnashing of teeth."* From this quote it would be easy to conclude that the price of not following the path of the Beatitudes is death.

As our efforts allow us to be brought into this state more often and for longer periods we will continue to experience a form of suffering. But this is not the same suffering experienced in the second Beatitude. What has happened is that much of the suffering experienced in the earlier stages results from our self-assigned guilt that is enhanced by our lower emotions. Now we can begin to see these lapses into waking sleep as a natural product of our lower nature and to some degree a lawful manifestation of natural processes. Suffering then becomes simply the payment, the effort, to remain vigilant. We cannot expect to stay awake for long periods and must physically sleep to allow our systems to be re-energized. In like manner, we do not have sufficient

---

[120] Matthew 25:14-30

The Fourth Beatitude – Gathering Truth

energy to remain awake or fully conscious for long periods and must expect that we will frequently fall back into our waking sleep.

To continue on the path we will have to strive to stay awake — vigilant — [our conscious labor] and endure our resistance and "unknowing" [intentional suffering]. We cannot overcome the resistance but in moments of being present, a higher energy, a special input of grace can lift us from its grasp. Our success will depend on the strength of our wish to be and our repeated efforts to allow the new, unfiltered knowledge to feed our higher nature.

We are immersed in a sea of truth. If we are awake, perhaps the impressions that carry the truth will not be blocked or taken and replaced by internal mental and emotional associations from our lower nature. The guidance, answers and help we seek await our willingness to drop our fixed ideas and accept the truth of this moment.

The Fourth Beatitude – Gathering Truth

Truth awaits all who can give up all they have — the knowledge, beliefs and habits stored in their lower nature.

The Fourth Beatitude – Gathering Truth

The Fifth Beatitude — Accepting Mercy

Blessed are the merciful, for they shall have mercy[121]

The literature is full of discussions of the desirability of and the methods for developing mercy. But try as we might, we will see that we cannot develop mercy on our own. It is a gift from above to those who have seen the truth of their own inner lives. It is given as an unmerited reward for our inner efforts of vigilance and not as a result of exterior actions. What can give the false illusion that we are merciful is often a small set of learned responses to a few select people under a few conditions.

---

[121] Matthew 5: 7 KJV.

The Fifth Beatitude – Accepting Mercy

Outside of those few situations, if someone steps on one of our "sensitive spots" we complain.

Honest self-observations will show that we do not appreciate the wonder of this creation that we are — we do not like ourselves — we have no self-love. That means we are not able to comply with the Golden rule to love others as we love ourselves. And while it may seem strange at first, the prime obstacle that blocks our love of ourselves is our self-love: our ego, vanity and pride that are the controlling part of our human nature.

The efforts to see our sleep and the illusions we have of our personal "goodness," will begin to challenge our ability to ridicule or assign blame to the actions of others. Seeing over and over the weakness and infrequency of our efforts, how can we blame anyone else or feel superior? From this inner ferment a space is created for the gift of mercy. Not by our effort to be merciful but by the effort of seeing that we are not merciful.

In rare moments we may see that each person has been programmed exactly as we were. The moral codes, cultural biases, and environmental conditions may produce widely varying results but those are in a certain

The Fifth Beatitude – Accepting Mercy

way as superficial as we have seen our own personalities to be. Maybe we have been gifted with a chance to awaken but it is only a chance for we must persist in traveling the path prescribed by Christ in the Beatitudes entirely alone — with help from above.

~~~

An exercise in listening

It may prove quite valuable, as an exercise, to try to become sincerely interested in listening to our self and others. The mechanisms that form words in us, whether spoken out loud or just internally provide an opportunity for real self-observation and study. And perhaps if we were able to listen, we might hear in another the same types of questions we have had along our journey even if others do not ask them in the same way or use the same words we have. This is a great and difficult experiment that we can try at any moment on ourselves and each time we are with others.

~~~

The Fifth Beatitude – Accepting Mercy

The most valuable yet difficult exercise we can try in this stage or any of the earlier stages is to bear the unpleasant manifestation of others that are directed at us without manifesting a negative reaction. Such actions from others are powerful assaults on ego, vanity and pride that call forth our immediate and often violent [at least inside] reactions. Such personal attacks often put us to sleep for days as we delight in reliving the experience by condemning the other and justifying our actions and reactions. Or we spend time with guilt and blame which puts us into sleep in exactly the same way. This identification drains and may completely eliminate the energy required for vigilance making it impossible to work.

However there are some ancient traditions that indicate that if we can resist the impulses to manifest a negative reaction, in time that negative energy can actually be converted into a force for our own benefit. But this is a very difficult exercise.

The Fifth Beatitude – Accepting Mercy

> *In reproving others there is no difficulty, but to receive reproof and allow it to have full course – this is difficult.*[122]

The fifth Beatitude is similar to the second in that it marks a wide plateau that may take quite a bit of time to cross. Now that we can return to ourselves and perhaps remain present more frequently, we will revisit this stage often. And we may not make it past this stage, for unless our egoism is substantially subdued we will go no further. And one of the most dangerous of the distractions provided by our ego is the thought that now "I" might be able to change the condition of mankind or at least help a few close friends and relatives. Here again the warning given by Christ is critical to our development.

> *But seek ye first the kingdom of God and His righteousness; and all these things shall be added unto you.*[123]

---

[122] Duke Mu, [Chinese Ruler of seventh Century BC], "Shu Ching, Book of Chou XXX"
[123] Matthew 6: 33 KJV

The Fifth Beatitude – Accepting Mercy

First we must awaken ourselves before it would be possible to awaken others. This may sound selfish but without the broad background of rightly conducted self-observation, the help we offer could do more harm than good and in certain cases could permanently prevent another individual from ever beginning their search. And the penalty for interfering with another's search is severe — severe enough to be repeated in three gospels. Christ warned that such people would have a millstone-tied around their-neck.[124]

Not only do we have to relinquish the idea that we are somehow already *nearer my God to thee* but before we can follow the indications of Christ we still have many of our perceived riches, the old ideas, the old tattered garments. This message is quite clear in Christ's parable of the wedding feast where those that were originally invited declined to attend. Not only did they decline but on the second invitation they even killed the King's son. And while this is a clear forewarning of Christ's own death at the hands of those he came to save, it also stands as stark reminder that being a member of any religion does not prevent us from being caught in our own ideas and

---

[124] Matthew 18: 6 ; Mark 9: 42 ; Luke 17: 2

The Fifth Beatitude – Accepting Mercy

beliefs and unwilling to be open to the invitation — the call. And for those invited guests for whom the king had prepared the feast that they could not accept, there was no mercy.[125]

> *Then he said to his servants, 'The banquet is ready, but those who were invited were unfit to come. That is why you must go out into the byroads, and invite to the wedding anyone you come upon.' The servants went out into the byroads and rounded up everyone they met, bad as well as good. This filled the wedding hall with banqueters.*[126]

Notice that the servants gathered those who were considered both evil and good. Mercy it would seem is not extended only to those considered by us to be good. The message here is that even though we see our limitations and inadequacies [the old concept that we are sinners] we still have a chance through the mercy of God.

> *But when the king came in to look over the dinner guests, he saw a man there who was not*

---

[125] Matthew 22:2-7
[126] Matthew 22:8-10 NAB

The Fifth Beatitude – Accepting Mercy

> *dressed in wedding clothes and he said to him, 'My friend, he said, how is it you came in here not properly dressed?' The man had nothing to say. The king then said to the attendants, 'Bind him hand and foot, and throw him out into the night to wait and grind his teeth.' The invited are many, the elect are few."*[127]

And even those who perhaps have travelled a way along the path of the Beatitudes, [having been invited and brought to the wedding] cannot escape the need to cast off the old garment [beliefs, habits, ideas] for unwillingness to do so leads to a rather terrible penalty.

The first five Beatitudes are concerned with this activity of casting off the "old." Exactly like the rich man we find it very difficult to accept the fact that all that we think we know must be set aside. But the challenge given the rich man appears to indicate that this seemingly enormous effort must be made before we can hope to hear, much less to follow Christ's guidance for us. And we are beginning to see that we cannot by our own effort accomplish this great work of shedding the old garments with which we have been tasked.

---

[127] Matthew 22:12-14 NAB

The Fifth Beatitude – Accepting Mercy

Here again we are given insight into the nature of what is required of us in these early stages. We are not asked to do any great external works in life, nor are we asked to give up our external riches but rather to remain vigilant. For with sufficient vigilance we will be shown right action.

Efforts up to now will have clearly shown that this "vigilance" is truly a great work requiring very much effort for we are going against the combined strength and determination of our egoism and personalities honed to near perfection for the entirety of our lives up to now. We must strive to strengthen our attention and our ability to stay present in the moment. Here again the message of Christ is clear. Even to those who had been following Christ, the apostles, in the Garden of Gethsemane he says "… could you not watch with me one hour?"[128] The ability to remain vigilant without distraction for an hour is an effort of truly heroic proportions.

And to conclude this section, it is useful to reflect on the strong connection between the gift of mercy and the

---

[128] Matthew 26:40

The Fifth Beatitude – Accepting Mercy

quality of humility. The origin of the word humility is from the Latin *humus*.[129] Humus is the substance resulting from the slow and lawful decomposition of rocks and organic matter.[130] The path of the Beatitudes is definitely about providing an opening to allow our inner selves to be worked. Work that can, if followed to the end, result in the death [and decomposition] of all that we are, all that we think we know and believe, and the emergence of our new selves as true, two-natured creatures of God.

This new self is not some sort of bland, weak being. We will retain our personalities, our knowledge and understanding, our flaws and our strengths. But if we continue on the path, we will gradually become more capable of being present in the moment and able to apply or constrain our reactions to outer and inner stimuli.

---

[129] "The Shorter Oxford English Dictionary" by William Little *etal* Claredon Press, Oxford 1978. Vol. I; pg. 997
[130] ibid Vol. I pg. 995

A Note on Attention

'Our' attention is the attention of our lower nature. It is actually comprised of three different and independent kinds of attention one for each of the three separate functions of the intellect, emotions and body. They act independently, are of different strengths and they act at greatly different speeds. We drive home while absorbed with thoughts or worries of the day only to be shocked as we turn safely into our driveway without a clue how we drove home. The attention of the body, acting separately took over the job while our intellect's attention was identified with [attracted by] its thoughts and the attention of the emotional faculty was also "on-the-loose." These three attentions of the lower nature, often acting independently, could not be expected to allow us to manifest a truly free will. A free will would require the intentional and harmonious participation of

A Note on Attention

all of our faculties [and their attentions] including our higher faculties.

We exist in this fragmented state without a free will because each system is doing its own thing. How could we ever manifest sufficient attention to merit awakening when we are so proud when our normal intellect manifests even a small degree of attention. It would be a rather amazing demonstration of the force of our attention if we could say something as short as the Lord's Prayer slowly allowing the meaning of each word to be felt without the arising of extraneous thoughts or feelings or unnecessary physical movements.

Our observations up to now will have shown us that our loss of presence is a direct result of the weakness and divergent functioning of our partial attentions. Unfortunately, what we call our normal attention — the attention of the lower intellect — that has been of some use in earlier stages will be of little use from now on for it is too weak and also situated as a part of our lower nature where ego can hold it captive. It does not have and cannot attain the endurance, power, speed or energy now required, for only the attention of a higher order has that capability. And it will be virtually impossible to

A Note on Attention

progress beyond this stage until we have been sufficiently emptied of ourselves to be able to receive this new attention. This higher attention which cannot be called "our attention" has been called a gift from God, the presence of the Holy Spirit, or simply as Jeanne de Salzmann says "a look from above"

The attention of our higher nature which opens us to a wider perspective is not to be confused with an ability to concentrate. Concentration, as the word implies focuses one or more of the "attentions" of our lower nature on one topic, activity or event to the exclusion of other impressions around us. Concentration although often valued in society for its ability to be productive citizens is most often a form of identification that narrows rather than broadens our awareness. How many times have we made the statement that we did not notice … because we were concentrating on …?

But we are not alone in our quest for this purer form of attention for we are given help. At times, especially during a period of quietly sitting in the morning before becoming active in our day, we may be made aware of an inflow of energy that seems like a current flowing into us or a light vibration, or it may simply feel like we are

A Note on Attention

seen or in the presence of something more than ourselves. This can be the initial evidence of an attention of a much higher order then the weak attention of our normal faculties. This new attention requires no effort on our part and yet if we have not made efforts to seek it out it will not be given. We can also observe that is does not come from or appear to be located near any of centers of the normal faculties of the lower nature. It has been described as being seen, held in the sight of higher forces or a feeling the presence of the Holy Spirit — of God.

The repeated experience of this finer energy will allow us to become a bit more open to it in the middle of our day as we try to remember to come back to ourselves. But in the beginning it is very weak and easily blocked because we are not open enough to receive it. And for the most part we fail to try in life, attempting to be present only in moments dedicated to meditation and prayer.

As stated earlier our worded prayers can only be enlivened if we can become awake. And if we are awake to see and listen for the voice of God we are in a

A Note on Attention

prayerful state where words are for the most part unnecessary and in some cases may even be distracting.

This new openness is a part of the conditions of the fifth Beatitude: blessed are the merciful. If we allow ourselves to open to this prayerful state — a state of presence — where the higher attention could manifest through us, we would see that we no longer need to "forgive" others for we see that they, like us, are only acting the way they were programmed — the way they were educated. This is the dawn of the gift of mercy where we begin to understand Christ's message from the cross.

> *Father forgive them; they do not know what they are doing.*[131]

---

[131] Luke 23 : 34

A Note on Attention

The Sixth Beatitude — A Second Greater Gift

We are now at the end of the second triad of the Beatitudes. The first triad began with learning to look inside which led to the inevitable sorrow at what was seen and the growth of a real wish to be made whole and then ending with our being made open to a great gift — the earth. In exactly the same way the second triad began with a widening of our observations to the truth of ourselves and the growth of conscience and a sense of *right-wise-ness* which led to the growth of humility and mercy based upon seeing the truth of our own condition. Now this triad ends with the sixth Beatitude which promises an even greater gift, one might said the ultimate reward — seeing God.

The Sixth Beatitude – A Second Greater Gift

> *Blessed are the pure in heart, for they shall see God*[132]

The sixth Beatitude speaks of purity of heart. But by now in our search we have seen enough to recognize that we are anything but pure. We have seen and continue to see how far we fall short of what we are capable of being: How our lower nature still carries us away into our conditioned habitual responses — waking sleep.

But one thing has been made more refined — purer, less adulterated. Our wish now seems to fill the entire space of our body. And perhaps the value of this refined and purified wish is more clearly seen by the wording of this Beatitude in the New American Bible.

> *Blest are the single-hearted for they shall see God.*[133]

This quality of the commitment called forth in this Beatitude is provided by Christ's response to one who wished to follow him ... but only after he took care of some personal business.

---

[132] Matthew 5:8 KJV.
[133] Matthew 5:8 NAB

The Sixth Beatitude – A Second Greater Gift

> *Whoever puts his hand to the plow but keeps looking back is unfit for the reign of God.*[134]

This does imply that we are called to walk away from our responsibilities in life although a few will be called to service in this way. Rather it is a clear statement that every action in life should be governed by an unflagging desire to awaken and to hear what is being asked of us just now — in this moment — and then to do it.

It is after repeated returns to and thru the steps of the early Beatitudes that one may begin to notice that the goal or wish for spiritual growth has undergone a change. It has moved away from the intellectual or emotional picture that was formed in the lower nature.

> *When the idea of my head becomes the wish of my heart*[135]

This wish of my heart is an experience of a feeling originating in our higher nature. It is a pure feeling

---

[134] Luke 9:62 NAB
[135] Gurdjieff, G. I. "Meetings with Remarkable Men" E. P. Dutton & Company, Inc. New York, 1963 pg. 158.

The Sixth Beatitude – A Second Greater Gift

without words, a perception of the truth of our calling. It is a manifestation of conscience; a real emotion; real desire and love of God. It can only be positive unlike the often sappy, sentimental or negative manifestations typical of the learned emotions of our lower nature. In a moment of presence, the whole of our being is filled by a strong desire for continuing this openness to a state far above our normal existence.

These moments of extreme clarity and a connection to a flow of energy much finer than we have experienced in the earlier stages cannot be summoned as was the awakening in earlier stages identified in the first five Beatitudes. For we can see that these moments are gifts completely undeserved. And yet there is something that we can recognize. Jean DeSalzmann, a close student of Gurdjieff states it perhaps most clearly when she said that in these moments we see that these gifts of pure presence are not of our doing. Yet something remains up to us. If we do not try, nothing will happen.

We must continue to try and remember to awaken; to be vigilant; to be more present. We must continue to try and strengthen our attention by more frequent attempts to make the moments last longer. The attempts for the most

The Sixth Beatitude – A Second Greater Gift

part will show that we cannot get past a certain quality of attention by our own efforts. But we cannot allow the intellect to simply accept this without repeated personal verification for to accept without sufficient proof will feed our ego at the expense of our future development. And beyond that, we need to strengthen what attention we do have in order to be able to allow the higher attention to enter. The problem is that many are unwilling to work like this for sufficient time without any sign of progress. They choose to quit and thus end their potential progress. We must be willing to accept the truth of our weakness and the sight of our normal personal manifestations as a continuing payment — an intentional acceptance of the suffering of ourselves.

If we can persist in our goal to be free from the control of our lower nature, we will begin to experience a connection with the higher part of ourselves which for now may be impressions from our higher nature or possibly a connection to even higher forces. It is not important which it might be. But it is of critical importance that we recognize the difference between these experiences and the impressions and energies that enter through our lower nature. If we are unsure of an experience, we cannot afford to analyze or make

The Sixth Beatitude – A Second Greater Gift

assumptions for those arise in the lower nature. We should simply set the experience aside without analysis.

At this sixth stage of development we may begin to experience many different "qualities" of this connection to higher energies. And the experiences will vary greatly from time to time and from person to person. A few have noticed simple feelings of connectedness or openness. A few sense this state as a moment of very intense energy often felt as intense light not seen through the eyes or an electric current or high frequency vibration traveling through the body. But to limit the experiences of this state to just these few examples is in a real sense to limit God. And the desire to try and repeat some of our pleasant experiences or even to seek experiences others have related or stories we have read is natural but most often arises from the ego. This natural desire of the lower nature to repeat experiences or match the experiences of others can completely block our openness and lead to imagination about all sorts of mystical experiences.

Intense experiences will of necessity be brief for our physical bodies cannot yet withstand that much energy and must dissipate it. Fortunately the natural safeguards

The Sixth Beatitude – A Second Greater Gift

built into our instinctive systems can prevent overload in much the same way that it prevents us from holding our breath too long. Some may simply drop back into waking sleep; others may even fall into physical sleep.

But we will carry the memory of the experience often without being able to explain it to anyone in a coherent form that they could understand. We should not discuss these experiences immediately either with others or even replay them within ourselves. We need to allow some time for the impressions [this food of the higher nature] to be properly digested by the parts of our higher nature. But even after that we have to guard these experiences and not share them with anyone unless they are at the same stage or further along or have been acting as a guide. It is worthwhile repeating the warning given by Christ.

> *Do not give what is holy to dogs or toss your pearls before swine. They will trample them under foot, at best, and perhaps even tear you to shreds.*[136]

---

[136] Matthew 7: 6. - Lamsa, George M. "Holy Bible From Ancient Eastern Manuscripts" A. J. Holman Company, Philadelphia, 19th printing. In a footnote to this passage states "Do not speak words of wisdom to fools" pg. 957

The Sixth Beatitude – A Second Greater Gift

If we discuss our observations with people who are not seeking, we will experience that which is warned above in the Bible; not in theory but in fact. This is not meant as a denigration of anyone but rather a realization of the simple truth that preparation is required before it is possible to "hear." The same condition the apostles faced before they were taught the Beatitudes. In a similar manner we should not discuss this internally as the experiences will be made ordinary by our lower nature which delights in explaining and categorizing. Recognizing moments when the lower nature is trying to relive and explain our experiences can be a very good reminder to try and wake up again.

~~~

Exercise

In order to allow an opening for an answer not provided by our lower nature, it can be useful to intentionally try to not say the first or second answer or response that arises in our daily interaction with others. These quick answers are the lower nature's automatic answers and even if they may be the "right" answer, it is a stimulus

The Sixth Beatitude – A Second Greater Gift

response action that closes rather than opens us and others. If we allow a little time, other answers might arise and we could actually and intentionally chose to respond from a moment of more presence.

Remembering to try in this way can show us much more about ourselves while allowing time for answers to arise from our higher nature. Our connection to this higher nature is so fragile that a stimulus-response answer provided by the lower nature will close the connection.

~~~

Despite reaching this stage occasionally, we see that we are still so easily caught by the automatism of the lower nature. St. Theresa of Avila often commented on the value of seeing our weakness at all stages of development for it alone is the one thing that can maintain our humility in the face of our egoistic desire to claim what has been seen as "my" accomplishment.

The Sixth Beatitude – A Second Greater Gift

The Seventh Beatitude — A Call to Peace

Blessed are the peacemakers, For they shall be called children of God[137]

In the literature and sermons on the Beatitudes, the seventh Beatitude is seldom the focus. For most, opportunities to be peacemakers in our external life are not often noticed. But for a person who has started to follow the path of the Beatitudes it becomes apparent that peace making must first be applied to the reconciling of the various parts within ourselves — balancing the pull of both of our natures and all of our functions.

---

[137] Matthew 5:9 KJV

The Seventh Beatitude – A Call to Peace

We can see this process in the body. Every position the body takes, every movement of an arm or leg requires the balance of opposing muscle groups — forces. On a physical level, this is peacemaking, the harmonizing of opposing forces. Our ability to exist in this world, even our ability to breath and the ability to pump blood throughout the body requires that this balancing be a continuous and dynamic process. At times this balance can be strong and certain and at other times precarious and uncertain.

Here again, the bodies inability to travel into the future and past allow the body to maintain a balance of all bodily functions in this moment and under these conditions. Fortunately for us this process is automatic in man as it is in all living creatures. One way to understand the goal of the Beatitudes is to see that before we can begin to intentionally serve God, we must bring our partially-developed, time-travelling intellect and emotions back into the present moment in order to allow all three functions to be properly balanced.

How much more effort will be required to balance all of our functions in both natures? Unlike the body's automatic and instinctual ability to maintain a balance,

The Seventh Beatitude – A Call to Peace

the balancing, the peacemaking of all of our parts can only be a result of the intentional action of a person who is awake. It can never become automatic or habitual.

Our experience shows that even when we try to make efforts to be present there is a continual conflict between the parts that wish to be awake, parts that want to justify our every action, parts that want to assign blame or guilt and the parts that just want to get absorbed in external activity. We have been shown this continuous inner conflict as we have been given more opportunities to observe our inner selves in different circumstances in life. It is the primary reason why it is essential that we make efforts to remain vigilant in all activities in our life.

With these observations will come an understanding on a very deep level that no one could possibly claim to be a peacemaker without first having an inner peace. And if our observations of our selves "in action" have not proved this to us, history is full of examples of people that history has labeled as peacemakers who have created more problems than they solved by trying to insert their own idea of a peaceful solution.

The Seventh Beatitude – A Call to Peace

Even with the enormous gifts of grace and energy that have been given to us through our higher nature we are not free from the distractions provided by outside impressions and the inner activities of our lower nature. In order to remain open to this awakening energy for longer periods, we must try to maintain a precarious balance between being trapped by the automatism of our lower nature and the desire to ignore the lower nature [the things of this earth] and be absorbed solely into our higher nature. Retreating into either nature is not why we were placed on earth.

And of course we will not succeed the majority of the time and we will find ourselves back asleep. For as with all the stages along the path of the Beatitudes, the reaching of each step is a gift. But it is a gift only to those who can remain vigilant and only for so long as we can remain vigilant. For those who can suffer to see that they, as in this case, cannot of themselves maintain the internal balance, the peace required, it is a gift.

The real conflict occurs in every moment of being awake and it is between our two natures — the sheep and the wolf. Here in this inner space is all that is required for us to work on this stage and these inner conditions were

The Seventh Beatitude – A Call to Peace

provided to us for our spiritual growth. It is in this internal struggle to make peace where we confront our own inability, our often forgotten wish, and our continual opportunity to wake up so that we can begin again to pay for our existence and perhaps begin to intentionally assist the creative plans of our Father.

A poem by Rumi[138] describes the challenge of making inner peace.

The Guest House[139]

> *This being human is a guest house*
> *Every morning a new arrival*
> *A joy, a depression, a meanness*
> *Some momentary awareness comes*
> *As an unexpected visitor.*
> *Welcome and entertain them all!*
> *Even if they're a cloud of sorrows*
> *Who violently sweep your house*
> *Empty of its furniture*
> *Still treat each guest honorably*
> *He may be clearing you out*

---

[138] Rumi : 13th-century Persian Muslim poet, jurist, theologian, Sufi mystic and founder of the Mevlevi Order of dervishes.
[139] Barks, Coleman translator, *The Essential Rumi*, Harper One, 2004, pg. 109

The Seventh Beatitude – A Call to Peace

For some new delight.
The dark thought, the shame, the malice
Meet them at the door laughing
And invite them in.
Be grateful for whoever comes
Because each has been sent
As a guide from Beyond.

Because of our automatism, we lack a practice of trying to see more of our current situation: the broader picture. Moments of becoming more present have widened our vision but still we lack the balanced awareness necessary to embrace both the yes and the no in each situation. Our cultural biases, education and moral codes all work against us in this attempt to expand our awareness to include the "sheep and the wolf." But until we can see and accept to stand between the parts that want and the parts that do not want in moments of being awake; we cannot claim to have or be able to manifest a free-will.

~~~

An exercise

A way to work with this is to try and improve our ability to listen. Listening is the intentional effort to be aware of

The Seventh Beatitude – A Call to Peace

the impressions that we receive — what we hear. We have tried to use listening in earlier stages to help us remember to try and to stay present longer. Now we add the effort to try and hear the meaning of what others are saying. To be sure we will observe our automatic arising distractions evoked by their choice of words, the emotional reaction to their state in the moment, and even a subconscious physical reaction to their posture and movements. This is an experiment in standing between our automatic nature and our desire to actively listen.

~~~

One common approach used in many cultures, study groups and religious practices is to try and stop thoughts. This seems quite logical if only superficially so because one of the first things we notice is that we are easily carried away, distracted by, or identified with our automatically arising thoughts. But these automatic thoughts are part of what can be measured as the background electrical activity of the brain. And eliminating them would mean eliminating that natural activity. The absence of brain activity is one definition of death.

St. Theresa of Avila even cautions against trying to stop thoughts because …

The Seventh Beatitude – A Call to Peace

"... the very care used not to think of anything will perhaps rouse the mind to think very much."[140]

What often passes for stopping thoughts is the experience of a moment when we are not caught by them. The goal is to be able to watch, to allow without changing anything. The unprocessed impression itself — what is being seen — is the real and necessary food for the growth of our conscience and consciousness. And at times we will be given a state where we can watch the thoughts running thru our normal intellect like clouds through the sky. But like clouds sometimes they are dark and thunderous and cause fear and at another time they may be shaped like a cute rabbit and we are fascinated by them [identification] and other times, if we can remain awake, they may become simply clouds passing overhead.

The idea of peacemaking, especially as spoken of in *The Guest House* above, includes the idea of acceptance. In this stage, we find ourselves more open to the reality of the world about us. Poverty exists and will continue.

---

[140] Teresa of Avila, "The Interior Castle," translation by Kavanaugh & Rodriguez, Paulist Press, New York, 1979, pg. 80

The Seventh Beatitude – A Call to Peace

Violence exists and will continue. Ego, bigotry, gluttony, each will remain as long as men remain one-natured beings. Each trait of human nature will be lawfully manifest in the world before us. However, having seen these traits and tendencies within ourselves, we can recognize and in a way accept their existence. This does not mean that we condone these conditions. Rather having seen the difficulty of overcoming them by ourselves we recognize the difficulty that others would experience in the same attempt.

The recognition of this truth creates within us a kind of impartiality to the events happening in the world about us. This compassionate impartiality recognizes a duty to assist others where possible but only when we see that the recipient is open to the help being offered.

We can however rest with faith and hope in the words of Christ that in time and with our effort to be open, we will experience this peace that surpasses understanding.

> *Peace I leave with you, my peace I give unto you: not as the world giveth, give I unto you.*

The Seventh Beatitude – A Call to Peace

Let not your heart be troubled, neither let it be afraid..[141]

But this "bequeath" awaits our openness. We have all been given an experience of a moment when, "shocked into a state of presence" by an inner conflict or external trauma, inner calm is experienced and we are simple able to be — to exist simply in the moment. Balanced between and freed from emotional extremes we feel a clearer sense of the reality about and within us. Freed from the constant hypnotic drone of the inner dialog of our normal mind we can remain in a quiet and observant place within. Freed from the adrenaline and the nervous physical activity, our bodies become calm and open to all of our senses. But this is only a brief foretaste of what awaits and the ability to be in the "eye of the hurricane" while staying calm and attentive is one model of that peace

A peacemaker must put aside attempts to eliminate inner parts and habits "we do not like" or "actions" we have been taught are evil and simply seek to become more "appropriate" in each moment. In some way it is in these moments of being opened that we are reconciled,

---

[141] John 14: 27 KJV

The Seventh Beatitude – A Call to Peace

brought into a condition of peace. The inner and outer conflicts we experience are part of the conditions that can enable our development. In many respects it is seeing our "sins" and bad habits that can fortify our wish to be free and sustain our real efforts. So we should not expect either inner or outer freedom from the opposing forces in life. Christ gives a direct indication of this in the little-quoted passage in the gospel of Matthew.

> *Do not suppose that my mission on earth is to spread peace. I have come to set a man at odds with his father, a daughter against her mother, and a daughter-in-law with her mother-in-law;*[142]

This quote is interesting in that it shows conflict between generations: younger against older. This might be a variation on the parable of the problem of putting new wine into old wine skins. For it is the new impression taken in during moments when we are more present that will challenge the old order within ourselves. In this lawful confrontation of the old beliefs and ideas with the truth seen in moments we are awake we can begin to get a clear picture of the concept of rebirth. The old system

---

[142] Matthew 10 : 34-38 NAB

The Seventh Beatitude – A Call to Peace

within us must die in order for the new to emerge. This is a real metamorphosis where like the caterpillar in the chrysalis all is dissolved in order for the butterfly to be formed and emerge.[143] To attempt to "blend" or "merge" or justify the differences will only strengthen our ego at the expense of our awakening.

There is also another sort of inner conflict that arises when we have a conflict between what our conscience says is right action and what our lower nature defines as "good." As mentioned before morality resides in the habits educated into the lower nature in childhood and conscience, the gift arising from moments of vigilance, resides in the higher nature. There is no better example of this sort of inner conflict than the story of Martha and Mary.[144] When Christ comes to visit their house Martha, having been taught how to be a good hostess immediately begins to prepare food and refreshment and is upset with Mary for not coming to help. Here is the lower nature trying to do what it and most cultures of the time considered to be good and becoming upset

---

[143] The metamorphosis of a caterpillar is a favorite example of the process of spiritual development used by St. Theresa of Avila.
[144] Luke 10: 38-42 NAB

The Seventh Beatitude – A Call to Peace

[judging] Mary for not following the same "rules of good hospitality." Christ tells Martha …

> *Martha, Martha, you are anxious and upset about many things; one thing only is required, Mary has chosen the better portion and she will not be deprived of it.*[145]

Notice that Christ does not say Martha is wrong; Mary simply has made the better choice. Martha's choice has led to her becoming tense — upset — closed.

Mary is "childlike" in her desire to stay with Christ. She acts like any young child attracted to something or in this case someone interesting. This is an inner struggle all adults face and it becomes increasingly hard to be childlike as we become more "educated," sophisticated and habitualized. For Mary, is able to forget the habits and education that have concretized Martha's view of how the world should be and focused on the new — the unknown — the miraculous.

This childlike state also contains a reminder of the necessity of vigilance, for in modern times, as soon as a

---

[145] Ibid 41-42

The Seventh Beatitude – A Call to Peace

child is introduced to television, music players, computers and game consoles, they begin to lose the "child-like" state. Before that, they are alert to everything around them, sensitive to people's moods, inquisitive, loving and playful. After they are introduced to these modern instruments they begin to lose contact with the world around them.

It is this story of Martha and Mary that allows us to see the connection in this Beatitude between inner peace and being made "children of God." And yet the goal of inner peace and the choice of wonderment over habit appears again in several of the gospels when the disciples were "trying to maintain order" in the crowd and trying to "protect" Jesus.

> But Jesus said, "Let the children alone, and do not hinder them from coming to Me; for the kingdom of heaven belongs to such as these."[146]

"…to such as these" belong the kingdom of heaven.

~~~

---

[146] Matthew 19:14; Luke 18:16

The Seventh Beatitude – A Call to Peace

If we occasionally reach this stage, we will see that the chaos or randomness of our outer life on earth can only serve to help remind us to come back into the moment and strengthen us in our journey. We must now accept more deeply that we do not know what to do in most cases and even when we do, we seldom have the strength of attention to accomplish any but the simplest of tasks without a gift of energy or help from above. But for those who occasionally reach this stage, there is an enormous advantage. Our own repeated personal experiences will have proven to us that the act of watching — observing in moments of presence — will allow the higher energy or grace to direct our steps and make the changes in us. This is exactly how the divine gift of faith can and will replace what had been only beliefs.

A quote from a poem by Seng Ts'an[147] reaffirms the requirement for inner peace if we are to truly follow what is required of us in this moment.

---

[147] Seng Ts'an: Jianzhi Sengcan (died 606) is known as the thirtieth Patriarch after Siddhārtha Gautama Buddha. Known as the putative author of the famous Chán poem, "Inscription on Faith in Mind"

The Seventh Beatitude – A Call to Peace

The Supreme Way is not difficult if only you do not pick and choose.
Neither love nor hate, and you will clearly understand.
Be off by a hair, and you are as far from it as heaven from earth.
If you want the Way to appear, be neither for nor against.
For and against opposing each other this is the mind's disease.
Without recognizing the mysterious principle it is useless to practice quietude.[148]

As we are given more experiences of an inner balance or harmony allowing us to remain inwardly quiet, we will begin to see more options in every situation. This can lead to the most stringent test of our wish to be present.

Being truly impartial can be a serious problem in a partial world.

---

[148] Seng Ts'an, "Inscription on Faith in Mind"

The Eighth Beatitude — Facing the Sheep and Wolf

We live in a "black and white" world where most actions and things are labeled "good or evil," "right or wrong" and this eight Beatitude warns that difficulties will arise.

> *Blessed are they that are persecuted for righteousness sake, for theirs is the kingdom of heaven*[149]

Every religion, cause, and philosophy, has stories of how the "true seeker" may face persecution for his or her beliefs. Fables relate how the hero and heroine must overcome great difficulties and trials.

---

[149] Matthew 5: 10 KJV.

The Eighth Beatitude – Facing the Sheep and the Wolf

Many, however, assume that the normal types of suffering encountered in our lives are the sufferings referred to in this Beatitude. The type of "accidental" suffering endured in our habitual waking sleep is seldom the persecution discussed in this Beatitude. Nor are we to assume that, like Christ and the early Christians, there will be some "evil" government or super human personification of "evil," that will oppress and torture us as we progress on our path of spiritual development. In life there will always be wars between races, cultures, families and misunderstood religious beliefs but these most often arise out of greed, ego, the desire for power and misinterpretation.

> *... and a man's foes will be they of his own household.*[150]

We see the truth of this Biblical quote in the life of Jesus who was attacked by the people he was born to save. Job is tormented in his time of loss by the comments of his closest friends and his wife. And there can be none closer to us than our inner personalities, education, ego, habits, and our "brilliant" thoughts — our inner household.

---

[150] Matthew 10 : 36 KJV

The Eighth Beatitude – Facing the Sheep and the Wolf

The ego, a member of our inner household, senses its loss of control and will resist with its last bit of strength. In ways that are cunning and shrewd, our own beliefs, habits, and fears will at times rise up to create an inner persecution to try and get us to retreat from our goal. In fact there is no greater adversary than our ego for it knows all our weaknesses, it knows our desires and habits, and it knows what we are seeing and thinking and how to put us to sleep with them.

It seems that Jonah faced this same inner dilemma when he reached a stage in his progression where he could hear God speak to him.[151] Jonah had become sufficiently open to hear what was being required of him. And his human nature naturally did not like the message. He did not want to do what he was being directed to do. So he struggled and was said to be in a "fish" a common idiom of the time. But it could be said in more modern terms that he was in a "pickle," "between a rock and a hard place" or in a "stew."

In this and other stories and legends we see that the "persecution" we receive will not necessarily come from

---

[151] Jonah 2: 1-8

The Eighth Beatitude – Facing the Sheep and the Wolf

afar. Friends, relatives, family members, and associates may become like Job's wife and friends. But the inner persecution will be even more challenging. All of our fixed ideas, all of our fears and prejudices will be thrown at us as if in one last great attempt to get us to fall back into sleep, and they will often win pushing us back into our conditioned, habitual response patterns.

In this conflict, depicted in fables and legends as a battle with dragons, ogres, evil spirits, the dark side, or the devil, the inappropriate traits and tendencies of our human nature are pitted many times against the brave and pure knight — our real self — our emerging "I." In Norse mythology it is Thor who battles the Midgard Serpent [his fixed ideas that are protecting the established world] which has grown so large that it completely encircles the earth seeking to maintain the old order and habits. In this and other myths, Thor or the knight is often beaten and wounded and must retire from the battle to heal before returning with new energy and more experience. In the myth of Thor, during the final battle both sides are destroyed and a new being arises. These stories are a surprisingly clear representation of our efforts in this stage. We are overcome by our habits and beliefs and continue to fall

The Eighth Beatitude – Facing the Sheep and the Wolf

back into our sleep. But like the heroes in the fables we must recover from our loss of awareness and awaken to return to the struggle.

But there are other less recognized forms that this persecution may take, and one of the more dangerous forms is when people speak well of you.

> *Woe to you when all speak well of you. Their fathers treated the false prophets in just this way.*[152]

St. Theresa of Avila also mentions this temptation.

> *In any case, to be well spoken of is only one trial more and a worse one than those already mentioned.*[153]

This particular challenge spoken of and experienced by St. Theresa may become ever more present as we arrive at these later stages of development. And there are many who have succumbed to the lure of compliments and

---

[152] Luke 6: 26 NAB
[153] St. Teresa of Avila, "Interior Castle" translated and edited by E. Allison Peers, Image Books, Garden City New York, 1961. Pg. 128

The Eighth Beatitude – Facing the Sheep and the Wolf

awards which re-energizes the ego, vanity and pride and causes us to fall back to sleep.

If we can continue to face into this inner and outer conflict between our emerging conscience [the perceiver of truth and righteousness] and the automatic manifestations of our lower nature as well as our outer life situations we will be saved. And exactly like the efforts in the second and fifth Beatitudes our time in this stage will depend on many factors and we will not be granted the grace to pass this stage until we are at last purified.

The Ninth Beatitude — The Search can Begin

The final statement of the Beatitudes is as follows.

> *Blessed are ye, when men shall revile you, and persecute you, and shall say all manner of evil against you falsely, for my sake. Rejoice, and be exceeding glad: for great is your reward in heaven: for so persecuted they the prophets which were before you.*[154]

Some commentators do not include this as a Beatitude even though it begins with the same words as the previous eight — Blessed." But this Beatitude represents the necessary culmination of the Path of the Beatitudes.

---

[154] Matthew 5 : 11-12 KJV

The Ninth Beatitude – The Search Can Begin

One might expect to see this final step as the fulfillment of the initial wish — completion — freedom from all of our "sins." Although this stage does represent the completion of the path of the Beatitudes, it has only served to prepare us to be able to fulfill our purpose on earth as conscious, two-natured human beings. It is the final step in accepting our God-given role. And as such, our goal may now become to intentionally allow the creative energy originating from God to pass thru us into the world and the impressions gathered through us to be sent back.

The good works we are tasked with do not imply that we will become miracle workers although some might. Most will never speak in tongues but a few will. It does not imply we will be great teachers or even respected leaders. And it does not mean that we will suddenly know all the answers — far from it. Hopefully, having been opened to receive, we will find, recognize and properly use our "spiritual gift."[155] But again, we cannot expect to understand our unique purpose and properly use our gifts until we have been prepared and sufficiently opened to allow it to be given to us. In fact

---

[155] 1 Cor. 12:4-11

The Ninth Beatitude – The Search Can Begin

some who have experienced receipt of one of the "spiritual gifts" before reaching this stage have also succumbed to their ego's hypnotic spell.

The good works may also be seen as one meaning of the parable of the talents.[156] For those who have prepared and continue to make efforts to be open, more will be given. And while we recognize that our efforts in following the way of the Beatitudes has been small compared to all that we have been given, we are told that much more will be given … if we can continue to strive to stay awake. And as the parable of the talents indicates, to do nothing will lead to our deaths.

This standing between both natures is a manifestation, a realization of our two-natured existence — the condition we were put on earth to experience. It is not anyone else's condition. It must be ours. It is not a condition we can hold up to the world to show our "exulted" achievement for that road leads to a certain kind of insanity. It is not our condition that we can experience when convenient or in special moments we have set aside for prayers. It must be our condition all of the time

---

[156] Matthew 25: 14-29

The Ninth Beatitude – The Search Can Begin

— in the middle of our lives. Efforts to this point have only helped to verify this. And yet in this realization, in this continued affront to our diminishing egos, lies our last and first real hope.

> *and he who does not take his own cross and follow me is not worthy of me.*[157]

The cross is considered by some to be a symbol of our two natures. The horizontal timber representing our human nature moving along in time from past to future while the vertical timber represents the possible scale of our being, the degree of our awareness, consciousness or connection to our higher nature which at each moment may be higher or lower. We are tasked to find a way to both join and balance these two natures — in this moment. Our preparation along the path of the Beatitudes has shown that the strength of that connection will always be proportional to the strength of our attention or perhaps more correctly, the attention that can flow through us. We will have to become increasingly proficient at maintaining this connection in the middle of life. And our permanent question will become "What is required of me just at this moment?"

---

[157] Matthew 10 : 34-38

The Ninth Beatitude – The Search Can Begin

But the answer will not be heard if we are asleep. And the suggestion we do hear while asleep will be from our lower nature.

The ninth Beatitude implies that we will face the continuous challenge of the normal distractions of life, our engrained habits, automatic reactions, and automatic justifications that are part of our human nature. This is our wolf. It is in this struggle that we can begin to reclaim our rightful inheritance as children of God.

We will not have reached "heaven" or perfection on earth following this great teaching. The Beatitudes were not designed for that. But rather having been raised to the ninth stage we have been given the opportunity to become fully alive and present to both of our natures. And from here we can begin to search for and intentionally accept the role foreordained for us on earth as an intentional conduit of a divine creative energy manifesting on earth and a returning energy flowing back into the universe. Our journey can begin.

~~~

The Ninth Beatitude – The Search Can Begin

Just now, at this moment, we can accept that we have been asleep and we can make the choice to start over — to awaken. That is the call of the Path of the Beatitudes.

From the Author

This project began in a fifth grade classroom. The topic was the Beatitudes. The Beatitudes were presented as a set of separate conditions in which a person might find themselves and the divine grace or gifts that would be given to the person under those conditions. Without knowing why, something seemed to be missing from this explanation.

Listening to these nine Beatitudes, I was bothered by the fact that those who sorrowed would be comforted while others inherited the earth for being meek. It seemed unfair! Some would see God while others only got a pat on the head — comforted. Of course I had my favorites, preferring to see God or inherit the earth way above simply being comforted or worse yet, persecuted.

From the Author

At that moment, the thoughts that flowed of their own momentum could only see the injustice and inequality of the various trials and rewards. As if to make the situation more confusing, there was no indication of how I might influence the decision over which I would receive and I was sure that there should be. This was a deep and weighty problem and clearly one of great importance to me at that moment. But then the school bell rang and it was off to recess: the question forgotten.

Fifteen years later the deep itch of a question without words was beginning to make itself felt — a question long blocked by developed habits, education, and the speed of life — a question about my purpose on earth and beyond which only seemed to grow bigger with time. Looking back, it is as if the question in the fifth grade was an early sign of questions that had silently sprouted and were now emerging into the light of my awareness although still faint and obscure.

The recurrence of this question and others, for which the published answers seemed somehow inadequate, only served to strengthen a conviction of a "something else" buried within me that was not being addressed. The sense of a missing connection to something bigger

From the Author

served to further strengthen these as yet unformed questions and began to lead me on a search through many areas.

In the beginning, my religious education appeared to only offer a path of beliefs that did not fit my wish to know why and how. Science with its experimental approach, although a first love, offered only a slightly closer approach. But science stopped when the phenomena could not be measured with available instruments or easily repeated. Conventional philosophy and theology ... well, a few dips into the weighty tomes proved that I, at that time, had insufficient discernment and experience to separate logical fact from equally logical sounding fiction in what appeared from my perspective to be a well-developed Babel.[158] Spiritualism and the related fields of the paranormal presented very definite and interesting possibilities and data.[159] However, after several years of searching and

---

[158] Babel was the ancient city in Shinar referred to in the Book of Genesis as the site of a tower whose building was interrupted by a confusion of tongues.

[159] Here paranormal is taken to include both psychic phenomena as well as what are called the Gifts of the Holy Spirit [1 Corinthians 12 : 9 – 10]

From the Author

experimenting in these areas, it became apparent that the very real — though rare — phenomena witnessed were, for me, non-reproducible in any fashion that could be learned. What's more, the individuals I encountered who seemed most able to manifest "unusual" phenomena and provide honest answers admitted that they were unable to teach others. For me, the overpowering emotionalism and vivid imagination of many people attracted to and enthralled by the people with these "psychic" abilities or "gifts of the Holy Spirit" was a distinct turn-off.

It was becoming clear that in order to understand more of the message contained in the Bible I needed to begin to better understand the meanings of the passages. Bible studies spoke of the geography, customs, history and the etymology[160] of the words. But this proved insufficient for me to uncover answers to my question of how.

Then after several years with a small group of friends with the same questions, we found and were guided by several people from the east to experiences of life in a different way. These experiences accumulated over more

---

[160] Etymology is the study of the history of words, their origins, and how their form and meaning have changed over time

From the Author

years formed the key that helped me to unlock some of the mysteries contained in the Bible and ultimately led to a deeper study of the Beatitudes. And as I have said several times earlier, I have no doubt that the Beatitudes supported by the other parables of Christ are the primary teaching of Christ. But I am equally sure that lacking a sufficient set of personal experiences, Christ's words and the directions contained in the Beatitudes will remain closed.

Observations

During my search, my respect has grown for those who are seriously involved in their own search. But I also have a growing conviction that many of these people are unaware of the much bigger tradition and body of knowledge that awaits those who continue to search. In many ways these were the people at the foot of René Dumaul's *"Mount Analogue."*[161]. In this story of search, many had endured years of preparation and the expensive and arduous trip to the remote island containing the mountain of truth. Having reached the

---

[161] Daumal, René, "Mount Analogue", The Penguin Metaphysical Library, Penguin Books Inc. Baltimore, MD 1952.

From the Author

island after much sacrifice, most of them had joined in to erect a town at the base of the mountain and were content to continue their lives there — at the base of the mountain. They had reached the island. And they were either satisfied to have reached the island, unwilling to make the extra effort to climb the mountain, or had never been told by their guides that the goal they sought could only be obtained atop the mountain.

In another story the same message is provided with more detail. This story called the Island of the Gods also includes a mountain.[162] The shoreline of the island is completely filled with boat docks and beautiful churches of every denomination line the shore. And as one might expect there are occasional confrontations between the people who attend the different churches. Further inland there are very old run down churches at the base of the mountain but few willing to walk that far even though they are within sight of all. The old Churches were thought to hold a strange belief that it is up to each person to actually climb the mountain of God.

---

[162] *Source unknown* Island of the Gods

From the Author

> *"Research" by very brilliant philosophers and religious scholars claim that from the ancient manuscripts uncovered near these old churches they are teaching contradictory messages – go east versus go west.*

Of course depending on what part of the island you were on — where you start — the mountain of God could actually be east or west or north or south. It depends on where you are at the moment you start.

> *People who have returned seem to be of two types. Most of those who start up the mountain return after not going very far and they are often quite emotional in their denial of any value [perhaps because they gave up] of the journey. Some of those who did not make it to the top of the mountain come back and start new churches where they tell others what they "saw" and why the views taught in the other shore churches are in err. Still others come back with a more peaceful presence but unable or unwilling to explain what the journey was like.*

~~~

From the Author

How we might follow our narrow path of the Beatitudes again brings us back to the need to see and accept that we have been asleep [to die to our beliefs and the ideas of personal accomplishments], awakening to a wider and brighter life [rebirth] and then becoming vigilant enough to hear and persistent enough to follow the directions we receive.

> *And I gave my heart to seek and search out by wisdom concerning all things that are done under heaven; to be engaged in it is a difficult task that God has given to the sons of men.*[163]

This God-given 'difficult task,' to seek out wisdom concerning all things — to climb the mountain of God — is one description of our purpose on earth. As Ecclesiastes continues it states that engaging in this task will lead us to see how all we are in our one-natured existence is the result of "vanity and vexation of spirit."[164] And yet this quote from Ecclesiastes only presents the difficulties of trying to free oneself from the habitual, the agreed upon knowledge, and the fixed ideas which bind and limit our search. It does not

---

[163] Ecclesiastes 1: 13 Holy Bible from Ancient Eastern Manuscripts
[164] Ecclesiastes 1: 14 ibid.

From the Author

mention the blessings that may come from the pursuit of wisdom. Our task, should we accept to follow the Path of the Beatitudes is the suffering— the sacrifice, the payment — required in order to be given the opportunity to share in the wonder and amazement of all things and to begin to intentionally participate in God's plan of creation. But the beauty of Christ's Beatitudes is that at each stage in the path we are told that we will be gifted with a bounty of grace or blessings.

Each moment of presence has the possibility of allowing finer impressions to enter us from life and perhaps to reach down to us from higher sources. Each new discovery, each bit of unfiltered personal experience we are given acts as another building block for creating a life of increasing faith. As new questions arise along the path we are provided an opportunity to apply that growing gift of faith with a certainty that the answers will be given … if and when we are sufficiently open to receive. Experiencing this growth of faith opens us to the gift of the cardinal virtue of hope. It grows organically, bit-by-bit from our search. And with each new discovery a person cannot help but be made open to receive another portion of the gift of Divine Love of all that is created and of all that has been given freely.

From the Author

But as has been repeated many times, it is essential that one not identify with the normal intellect's intrusions that modify or completely destroy the pure impressions. Each of us must suspend our automatic reliance on our partial understanding and knowledge in order to be open to what is new in this moment.

This is a task that is almost impossible until we can become a bit dissatisfied with our current state and the limitations imposed upon our lives by our fixed ideas. This dissatisfaction with our condition or the growing belief that something is missing in us is what could be called a precondition or an early indication of our approach to the path of the Beatitudes. If we begin to travel the path with a sincere desire to awaken we will begin to see that it is possible to be vigilant, to observe ourselves and our external condition with growing impartiality.

Continuing to try and observe ourselves impartially, we may in time begin to notice that a totally new kind of "knowing" begins to emerge: A perception of truth in the moment that does not arise from the normal intellect and stored memories. This is the dawn of the gift of wisdom, direct perception of truth in this moment. And

From the Author

wisdom comes as a gift from and through higher faculties that are a part of our spiritual nature. While our normal understanding arises through the integration of, the balance of, intellectual knowledge and practical experience, wisdom coming from above does not depend upon our understanding and in some cases can contradict our partial understanding. For this reason, wisdom, which is a gift from above, surpasses understanding. But to recognize such wisdom we must have been made unsure of ourselves and opened to receive.

Repeating something stated earlier, our great effort to awaken as defined in the Beatitudes can be benefitted through the help of a like-minded, small group of people working together in a very practical way. Working alone we are seldom able to notice our sleep, remember our wish to awaken and in our sleep often dream that we are awake. But with a group, there is a chance that one or another person in the group might be awake and by their presence alone remind the others. The odds are further improved if one person in the group is just a bit further along the path.

From the Author

This is not a group for the sharing of knowledge, speculation or past experiences like many psychological interaction groups. It is not a group for intellectual study of ideas and theories. It should not require any assumptions or beliefs. Instead, if properly formed, these groups will rely on the honesty of its members and their wish to awaken.

These groups are dedicated to sharing actual impressions, free from analysis: Impressions that have been gathered in moments of presence. This is what sets a serious group seeking spiritual development apart from other groups. Personal development requires personal and practical effort. In this effort our biggest obstacle will prove to be the strength of our beliefs and unsubstantiated knowledge.

In the end, it is the strength of our wish to be made open and our persistence in the search for truth, truth in this moment, which will allow us to be opened to receive the divine inheritance which is God's wish for each of us.

From the Author

~~~

The teachings contained in the Beatitudes can help guide that search.

www.ingramcontent.com/pod-product-compliance
Lightning Source LLC
Chambersburg PA
CBHW071354290426
44108CB00014B/1539